LIFE
Goes Both
WAYS

WILLY VIL

Copyright © 2024 Willy Vil
All rights reserved
First Edition

Fulton Books
Meadville, PA

Published by Fulton Books 2024

ISBN 979-8-89221-300-4 (paperback)
ISBN 979-8-89427-605-2 (hardcover)
ISBN 979-8-89221-301-1 (digital)

Printed in the United States of America

ACKNOWLEDGMENTS

I want to take a moment to express my sincere gratitude to everyone who has supported me in the creation of this book. First and foremost, I want to thank my amazing wife, Anelia, for her exceptional support in the development of the book. She read the early drafts, suggested and gave me advice on the cover, and kept the kids out of my hair so that I could focus on editing. Anelia, thank you so much for all that you do.

I also want to extend a special thank you to my three sons—Jacelay, Marley, and Widley. Marley helped me with the beautiful logo on the cover, Jacelay was with me from the start to the end of the process, and Widley kept us all grounded and relaxed with his humor. I applaud and acknowledge you all for a job well done.

To my friends and family who supported and believed in my abilities throughout the whole process, I express my deepest appreciation and sympathy. Your love and support mean the world to me.

A grateful thank-you to most of the teachers who gave me excellent advice while I was attending Purdue Global University. Because of you, I can write a book regarding everything that I learned from you. Don't feel left out if I don't mention your names because you know exactly who you are—great school and awesome professors teaching the students great stuff in the school.

Lastly, I want to thank everyone on the publishing team who has helped me along the way. You have all done an outstanding job, and I could not have done this without you. Special thanks to Jennifer Potoski at Fulton Books, the review board and Brandi Hayes, my amazing publication assistant and the greatest cover designer I could ever imagine. Thank you all once again for your support and encouragement.

Best regards!

Can you imagine how difficult it is for an immigrant to leave behind the people he loves, like his parents and friends, to reside in another country, especially in America?

It has been a long journey and a huge transition for me in the United States of America. After I graduated high school at the age of nineteen years old, I left the Caribbean to come to America. I lived with my oldest brother, John, in Brooklyn, New York, for about two months as things didn't work out well for us. A few months later, I moved to an area called Nyack, New York, which is approximately an hour away from Brooklyn. There I stayed with my three cousins—Jean, Chloe, and Marie. I bounced back from job to job as I didn't like them at all. When I was living with my parents in the Caribbean, I was not accustomed to going to work. My mother and servants used to cook, clean, and wash my clothes. Thus, I was not ready to live in America as my life was pretty sad for a long time. I was away from my family and friends, and English was my second language.

In the year of 1997, I went back to school just to set myself up for a better future. Going back to school though was not easy at all, so much so with language barriers. I was not getting good grades as I tried to translate French into English. When things were not going as planned, I dropped out of school and continued to work in order to support myself. Apparently, I was not happy with the direction my life was going through, but I decided to give school another chance (i.e., try again). In 2005, I went to a local community college, and I registered for a couple classes. There I met a terrific teacher who used to teach English at a prestigious university in France. That terrific teacher took the time in her busy schedule to teach me how to write essays in the English language. Like I mentioned before, English was my second language. She gave nice words of encouragement for feedback. Moreover, she told me that I wrote my essays in a philosophical manner, which was not suitable for the class I was taking at the time. The minute I put her advice into perspective, I was getting grades like As and Bs.

After a few years, I was able to get an AAS degree in business entrepreneurial finance with a 3.5 GPA. Thanks to that awesome teacher that I met at a local community college in Upstate New York, I was able to turn my life around quite a bit and accomplish something. From that point on, I started another chapter of my life. I got married, and as my wife and I were raising three wonderful boys, school was not a number 1 priority for me. We had mortgages and lots of other bills to pay every month. My focus was mostly on the kids and the bills. Now that all my kids are grown-ups who graduated from college with successful careers, I decided to do a major thing for myself. I decided to take care of unfinished business.

Back in August of 2021, during the pandemic, there were not that many things to do; therefore, I decided to go back to school to get my bachelor's degree in business administration management. I registered online at Purdue University Global for twelve credits. Before the semester was over, I was having As all across the board as I was unstoppable for three consecutive semesters. I made the chancellor's list five times, and I received an invitation from the National Society of Leadership and Success. I continued to have straight As and 4.0 GPAs at the age of fifty-plus years, and I graduated with a perfect 4.0 GPA. It's not for any apparent reason that I am telling you all these things. The main reason is to tell you that it's never too late for anyone to accomplish anything you desire in life or to perhaps chase your dream. The message I am trying to relate is that, if at fifty-plus years, I managed to have a 4.0 GPA till graduation, so can you out there. I hope that my journey will inspire and motivate lots of you out there. Additionally, I always wanted to inspire and motivate my children by setting vivid examples, like this particular instance where I think that I accomplished something huge in my life. Throughout my journey at Purdue University Global, I was so eager to share with you all the homework and grades that I received from those classes.

I truly hope they can help and motivate you towards anything you want to pursue in life.

When I came to America thirty-plus years ago, I thought that everything was going to be easy. I told my mother that I was going to be rich in the USA in no time. I was smart in high school, but I didn't have a plan of how to perceive life. It took me a lot of years to understand that my perception of life in the US was the opposite from what I previously thought. And I didn't have a mentor to guide me in the right direction. Both my mother and father were living far away from me in another country. Indeed, one of the ultimate ways to be successful in America was to go to school, work hard, and then invest money as soon as you have the chance to do so. To my knowledge, these are the clear-cut ways to make it in this country, unless, of course, you inherited a large sum of money from your family or you take certain risks that would eventually get you in trouble with the law.

Now that I am getting older and wiser and educated, I want to share some of my experiences with you. Today I can honestly sit down and be proud of myself and what I have accomplished in life so far. At fifty-five years, I just graduated from Purdue University Global at the top of my class (4.0 GPA). This is not an easy endeavor for someone like me as English is my second language. The reason why I am saying all this is to motivate others out there that have probably been in similar scenarios and have no idea how to proceed with their lives. I want to assure you that you need to have a vision and a good mentor. Thus, believe in your dreams and be ready to work hard to turn your dreams into reality. I am here today, and who knows that tomorrow would be you sharing similar stories and success. All you need is perseverance in life, and when life is throwing some curveballs at you, there is no need to discourage; work harder because someday you will see things in a different light.

In this journey, you will have the opportunity to read a lot of interesting homework regarding my assignments, and the grades were phenomenal. As a previous student, I had been struggling and fighting for the same things that some of you are trying to accomplish right now. During my time at Purdue University Global, I assembled a series of homework assignments, summaries of the courses, and grades for you to view. After reading them, you can form your own opinion and possibly learn a few things yourself. By contrast, I think America is still a great country to live in, and despite what some other people might say, the American dream is still standing in full force as it is never too late for anyone to succeed or follow their dreams. Besides, don't let anyone dictate or dare you about the things you can or can't do.

At various times in life, it depends on how badly someone needs to reach or accomplish a particular goal. Based on my recent experience, I can assure you that if you are committed and willing to work hard, the sky's the limit. For the vast majority of the time, all you need is a plan and to be disciplined enough to work toward your objectives. If you stay positive and don't sweat it, in the end, you can do it.

I understand that going to school, working, and keeping life balanced can be extremely hard, but when you reach your destination, the rest would be history. All the struggles would be forgotten when you finally cross the finish lines. When that happens, don't mind the haters, but instead, get ready to celebrate and enjoy your accomplishment. If I can do it at my age, so can you. I always believed in my abilities, but I never knew that I was capable of going back to school and graduating with a 4.0 GPA, especially at my age and a bunch of other factors. Eventually, I did all this to prove a point to my children. Sometimes, instead of playing video games, watching TV, etc., I would suggest that you register online or at a local community college for a class or two just to challenge yourself. No matter what happens, you are going to learn something, period. Another thing is, don't get comfortable as I advise you to stand up and challenge yourself by doing something constructive in your life. For instance, register for three or six credits at an accredited college or university toward something useful. Before you realize it, you will have all the credits necessary for an associate or bachelor's degree or something else. You may ask yourself this question: what the heck is he talking about? Well, I think that I am qualified enough to tell you that—I just got my bachelor's degree by doing the same thing I am telling you about. In parenthesis, I always feel fascinated about motivating people as a career because I sense that I can have a great impact on other people's lives.

Due to what I had gone through, I can attest that life is not easy. As always, great things happen for people who are determined, devoted, and work hard. When you reach that level of success, people will hate you, but they will show some respect. At various times, life is not as difficult as some people imagine it. Thus, if anybody applies the notion of "You have to work hard with the sweat of your foreheads to eat," I am certain that you will come to a better understanding that success goes toward people who sacrifice themselves for the sake of reaching their objectives. I suggest that you stand up and challenge yourself by doing something constructive with your life. For instance, instead of sitting in front of the television playing video games and anything else, I encourage you to go to a community college near you or register at a university online for just one class, not two or three, before you even realize you will accumulate enough credits for either a certificate or associate degree. Some folks may ask, What is he talking about? Well, I just completed my bachelor's degree by doing the same thing I am telling you right now. In parenthesis, I always feel fascinated about motivating others as a career as I have a lot to teach them. Like I mentioned earlier, I would like to share with you some of my works, assignments, initial posts, and responses to my peers from Purdue University. Most of those works led to very good grades. For instance, appendix A was one of my assignments.

Here is an assignment to write a letter to the HR department regarding employee's orientation and how to deal with customers. It's my pleasure to share it with you. Kindly see appendix B.

I always thought that it was an excellent idea to put together all my wonderful memories and essays and my experiences into a book. The reason behind all this is to inspire other folks or students to put all the negative thoughts behind them and to just follow their dreams to the paths of a successful future. If I can do it, so can you. Before I was able to accomplish all these things, I failed various times in my life that led to discouragement and great concerns for myself. With the help of friends and family and the great divine, I am able to stand up before you to talk about my journey at Purdue University Global. I would not change anything about the situation as it's been so far, so good.

Appendix C was an idea about one of the great assignments that I had assembled while I was at Purdue University Global. You're going to have plenty of time to read various essays, posts and answers to my peers' posts and questions. Without further ado, here is another one—please turn to appendix D.

For example, here is another assignment that showcases how important it is for someone to invest money in his or her life. Investing is particularly essential when it comes to making money. Accomplishing it wisely can transform your life for good. When you invest carelessly, it can have harmful effects on the investor. That's why it is essential to make sure you glance at all the probable curves of an investment. For instance, we will be examining an investment option that could make us a lot of money. In that instance, we were an investor in Angel, and we were operating with an entrepreneur as debt financing would usually concern two parties, but there could be others as well. You can read my essay on Appendix E.

I hope you are enjoying all the contents, advice, and experiences that I am sharing with you. This time I am ready to share some more assignments with you. My essay on Appendix F is one about human resource management role and description.

This one was a memo by me to human resource management. Please see appendix G.

On this assignment, we will be talking about motivation. Please see appendix H.

This particular moment, I am going to share with you one of my journal assignments. However, to avoid controversy and other problems, I am going to erase the professor's name as well as my name on the assignment. Without any further details, please see appendix I.

This is an assignment written in April of last year, 2022. As the assignment is unfolding, you will discover how I expressed myself on the subject of virtue ethics. Ladies and gentlemen, please refer to appendix J.

Right now you are going to have to read another assignment. It is from a class called MT 302: Organization Behavioral. This is a case study about motivation in the workplace. Please see appendix K. I hope you enjoy reading it.

Found in appendix L is a very interesting assignment regarding orientation when first getting hired at an organization.

APPENDIX A

Semtell Company: Cincinnati, Ohio,
November 15, 2022
Karl Richland-CFO

    Cash is how much money is coming in and out. On a cash-flow statement, you will see that getting money out is only one part of the equation. Bringing in a ton of money is huge, but keeping the expenses down is just as important. Advertisement expenses on the statements can be one of the major expenses for businesses and, if not taken care of accordingly, can eat up a good portion of the profits. It's crucial to monitor advertising costs and optimize campaign sales to make sure they are bringing in a positive return on investment. Advertisement/inventory costs can add up and take money away from even positive numbers. Indeed, short-term/long-term liabilities could be greater than the amount of money you are pulling in, resulting in less cash.

    Account receivable is how much money you will receive in the future. Accounts receivable will mostly be money owed to us by our customers. If our account receivable is decreasing, this is a great sign for us. Account receivable decreases when customers pay off their debts. This would mean that instead of I.O.Us; we would have substantial cash on hand. An increase in the inventory proportions would be a negative on the business. Inventory is where we store our items. The balance of the inventory lets us know how well we are selling our products compared to how many of our products we are purchasing. An increase in our inventory balance would suggest that we have more products in our inventory than we are selling them. That would be bad for the cash-flow statement because we are spending more money than we are making. That is an issue we should try our hardest to avoid because it could force some measures that would lose us a lot of money.

Asset account increases are a little tough. Many would think that if our assets are increasing, that would mean we are making more money but this is not the truth. Because the assets are increasing, you will need to spend more money on them, which will reduce the amount of cash at hand/cash flow. Liability accounts are similar in consideration. Many would assume that an increase in a liability account would be bad for a business, but that isn't necessarily true. If the liability account is increasing, that means that you have not used cash towards it. That means you could use that cash at hand towards other aspects of the business, which could pay off more than decreasing your liabilities.

Account payable is similar to liability accounts. Account payable refers to liabilities that the company needs to pay off. If the account payable is decreasing, that means the company is using a lot of cash at hand, which is bad for cash flow. If the account payable is increasing, it means that the cash the company has is being used for items that could bring more cash at hand.

There are two possible solutions I would offer for a working capital issue. First, we let our account payable balance increase. If we are using less money on paying off our liabilities, we could focus on different aspects of the business. If we do that, we could make enough money where we can pay off our account payable balance. Another solution I would offer would be to decrease the inventory balance. I would suggest we stop buying so many products and think about switching our inventory method. We should wait for customers to make requests for items, so we can see where the demand is. With less money going toward inventory, we could increase the amount of cash we have at hand.

There are many different ways that a cash-flow statement can help out a business. It can demonstrate how we are making our money, and where our cash is going. When you have a limited amount of working capital, it's important to note that there are ways around it such as limiting accounts like inventory or accounts payable.

From a cultural point of view, it is a very hard decision to undertake when you have to move your business, managers, family and employees overseas. There may be a lot of problems involved in that process. For instance, their alteration to the new climate may disturb the employee's capacity to operate well overseas. Another one is the language barrier. At last, they worry about how to make friends.

To improve the hiring process, there are many things that could have been done. The first thing they could have done was look for employees with overseas experiences. This way, the employees would be more prepared and have a better understanding of what to do. Another thing they could do is look for people who speak the language, and the culture of India. People who understand the culture would have a better understanding of the Indian's system and probably be efficient and more productive at their new positions. Lastly, I would make sure I ask human resources to hire a bilingual Indian expect in business and labor law who can help the transition with the transition procedures

In the process of moving employees overseas whether it is to expand the business or short-term business trip, Human Resource Management must be diligent to prepare them for success. In foreign lands, managers and employees are the ones that are going to work, and they're going to need a lot of support from the company and Human Resource Management. After all, they were chosen by the company to migrate elsewhere.

In this scenario the capable managers and employees that the company has chosen must make certain their effort isn't for nothing. The organization or HRM must make sure that the procedure is easy and that effort contributed by your team and the departers are up-to-date. Additionally, HRM may consider preparing emigrant managers and employees for overseas positions. For example, pre-move training, providing support on the ground and ensuring continued communication, invest in knowledge management. The training must be well organized by putting in perspective all the problems that they are going to face in India.

Though, the company should try to work with Professional Employer Organizations in order to make the transition easy. As far as cultural differences are concerned this proposition may be one of the solutions that can help a lot. Another area may be language training. No matter how fluent your migrant managers and employees may be in the foreign language it is worthwhile setting them up for local language training. It is absolutely worth getting them some help with the basics. This is an area that may be a great help to HRM or the organization. When you can't communicate with another peer it can create a lot of tension. Therefore, being productive at work for both managers and employees combined is really a big deal.

If I were Jorge I would ask Human Resource Management to get the employees all the help and support they need just to be successful in their transition. It is not easy to move overseas whether as a manager, employee, or with your family. They're too many things at stake. Indeed, being away from your own land, your friends, and your family while worrying about your financial future is a stressful situation for anyone. As Jorge, I would definitely get the managers and employees to a local training school to learn the foreign language. In addition, I would ask HR to hire some locals who are fluent in English to fill some positions. Lastly, I would go and have monthly checkups with the employee's family and explain how everyone is adjusting. Whatever I can do on my end to make their staying overseas a success I would do.

Footnote:

One of the biggest mistakes I see employers make is how they treat their workers. I understand that employees may seem like the least important aspect of the business but they can help the organization be the reason they advance or not. In fact, I worked various jobs and I have different opinions depending on how the employer treated/respected his employee. It's important to keep your employees happy; otherwise your business could end up crumbling down.

The company I have chosen is a corning corporation. It is an American intercontinental technology company that specializes in specialty glass, ceramics, and similar components and technologies among different items foremost optics, mainly for industrial and scientific utilization.

Right now is an excellent opportunity for the company to expand its product. Corning is focused on making many things, but they brag that their glass is second to none. That's why it would be a good option to make Corning Cups. That will be good for two reasons. First, because they are making glass, there will not be much more effort in making it. Second, because they are in the global market, they can expand their brand names and attract individuals to their various products. They should make glass cups with the logo of the company on them. At last, set them up in places close to the US market like Canada and Mexico.

Joining the global market will not be easy based on the diamond of national competitive advantage. In this model, many factors would prevent most companies from entering the international market. Because we are an established business with a lot of resources, many of these factors will not affect us. The two factors that we would need to watch out for are the government and other competitors. The cup industry is very large. There will be plenty of rivals as it is important to buy an established business so we can begin with their existing clients. The government part can be tricky depending on where we decide to sell our cups. I think that we should research countries where the government doesn't interfere with businesses such as Canada.

The company must expand in the international market. Due to Corning Corporation's resources globally they're a leader in the business of fiber optic communications system clarifications for voice, data, and video network functions internationally. For instance, fiber is approved over electrical cabling when high bandwidth, long distance, or immunity to electromagnetic background is required. This type of conversation can transmit voice, and video, and tell a story over local area networks or cross long distances.

When it comes to the importance of policies and procedures to the effective facilitation of strategy execution. The policy diminishes anxiety in repeated and daily actions in the control of critical strategy execution. Therefore, the policy restricts absolute movement and elective choices and performance. Procedures authorize steps on how kinds of stuff are to be managed. Finally, it regulates actions and practices with a strategy.

Associating a company's strategy to execution is important to accomplishing the organization's activity and conversion aspirations. In the absence of a durable association between the two, a company is running the risk of wasting time, attempts, and money on plans that will never lead to the predicted conclusion.

Concentrating on important processes and developments concerning the company that will help execute its goals. Eventually, make sure that communicating the strategy all across the business is appropriate. Additionally, engaging with employees and stakeholders, paying attention to criticism, and making sure that the right individuals have the means in place to help in their achievements.

One thing we will need to focus on will be the company's culture. Company culture is its values and how it affects the workplace. This is extremely important because this is what inspires/demotivates workers. If a company's civilization is not good, it will prevent employees from working their hardest. To maintain a good culture, there are two main things we should keep in mind. First, any form of power abuse will result in firing, no questions asked. Second, we will make sure that any sort of harassment will transform into a permanent suspension. We want our employees to be safe. If the company's culture becomes toxic, we will take action to revert that. First, we will have an interview with every employee in the workplace to figure out if anyone has made any awkward comments or if it's just the whole staff in general. We will get rid of any of the staff that we find to be disruptive. At last, he would be fired and banned from the company.

Another important thing that we will need is excellent leadership. Organizational leadership will be huge for our surgeries to work. Managerial leadership involves setting objectives to achieve something like budget and enhance execution. If we are setting goals to motivate employees to follow our strategy, it will increase the possibility that the strategy will blossom. Plus if employees are hitting attainable goals rather than a big objective, it will improve the company's morale and the culture.

As the team leader, it is important to make things comfortable for the teams. In this situation, you are working with individuals you are not familiar with, which can be a huge challenge to do. It is important to try various things such as creating a schedule that works for everyone, deciding on roles, and building trust. Powerful leaders aid or direct their group in the proper place. They have a good understanding of how to communicate, influence, and share a common objective with people concerning the bigger image. In this situation leading by example would be an ideal way to help the group get through this task. During this assignment, we will look at how we can operate in a group and how we can make the best decisions.

One thing that is important in a group is how they solve problems. One framework that is very straightforward to use is the P-MOPS. According to the book (Adams et al., 2021), P-MOPS, or the Procedural Model of Problem Solving is a "flexible framework that can guide each phase of problem-solving". P-MOPS is divided into five different stages. The first one is describing the problem and looking at it by yourself or in a group setting. This step may not seem very important but doing this is problematic for solving a crisis. When you are describing the problem in a group's surroundings, it makes it easier to see any potential issue with the situation. Thus, it gives your group the chance to toss out answers that may or may not be suitable. That will showcase the group's capacity to break down problems. The next step of P-MOPS is developing and presenting possible solutions. That can be referred to as the brainstorming stage. The group will think of any conceivable situation that could help with the situation. That will give each team member a better understanding of the problem and could flash some possible ideas for group members to operate on. That could also lead to members combining solutions to make better ones. The third aspect of this stage is glancing at and rating which resolution is the best and most harmful. That stage is important as it allows the team members to give their thoughts on the probable solutions. That could be a good way to talk about the negative aspects of the solutions and perhaps suggest a way to strengthen that explanation. The next stage is choosing the best resolution. The stage requires the most teamwork as the group needs to come together to pick a solution that best serves the group. That will require everyone to be on the same page and come to an agreement on one resolution. The last stage is taking that solution and executing it. That stage will require different types of teamwork as you need to understand who has the best skill set and put them in a role that makes them successful or the best way for that solution to work. P-MOPS is great for solving problems because it puts a certain framework for issues and gives details/simple ways to solve them. P-MOPS would be my first option for a framework for making decisions in a group because it is extremely effective and is split into stages to make it easier for them to organize their thoughts.

Decision tools are items that assist you with decision-making based on information from the book (Adams et al., 2021). That is important in group surroundings because it improves your chances of a successful decision being made. One decision tool that would be extremely helpful is a SWOT. SWOT stands for Strengths, Weaknesses, Opportunities, and Threats (Adams et al., 2021); which is very important for understanding what your team is good at. If you can understand what your group members are good and bad at, it allows you to put them in roles in which they have the highest chance of achieving. Another great tool when it comes to decision-making is an affinity diagram. Affinity diagrams are when you take information about a decision and put them into different sections of a diagram. That will highlight any potential patterns that may be necessary when you are making a decision. Lastly, we have the break-even map as a good decision tool for making decisions. That tool is only useful in problems in the business setting, but it is a good way to make conclusions. The break-even tool reveals how much probable solutions would cost and how well that answer would have to work for them or at least break even. That will permit you to make findings that are not pouting that company in debt and allows them to make the most money possible.

Now that we have the tools for success and the framework to make decisions, we can apply them to the problem that we have above. As the team leader, making things comfortable for the teams is essential. In this situation, you are working with people you are not familiar with, which can be a tremendous challenge. It is essential to test different things in this case such as making a schedule that works for everyone, deciding on roles, and building confidence. During the first group meeting, we will be doing two things. The first half of the meeting will be spent by each member making their SWOT. Nobody in this group is familiar with one another, so we will be learning more about each other. SWOT lets me see what they are good at, their weaknesses, and what are their goals/dreams. That works as an icebreaker and will build some trust within the team. The next half of the meeting will be spent using the P-MOPS stages. We will look at the problem and discuss everything about it. "The town (population 70,000) wants to have this annual celebration like it does every year. Thus, this year the town is short of funds, and the mayor has asked your 6-member committee (including yourself) to come up with a plan of action for implementation. We are now on September 10th." One thing I would note is the lack of funds. How could we go around this? Another thing to mention is that we have a little bit of time to think of solutions as we have to figure out the problem and solve it by December 10th. As we finish up discussing the problem, I would like to underline one major thing for the next meeting. First, I would try to make a schedule that functions for everyone in the group. Indeed, many people in the group are doing something like being with their children, so we must be able to work jointly. Once we assemble the schedule, I would get set for the next meeting. For the first half of the meeting, I will have everyone help me form an affinity diagram. We would break down the situation similar to how we did during the first meeting by writing down essential details and putting the identical report together with each other. Next, we would employ this diagram when we are brainstorming ideas, which will be what we do for the rest of the meeting. I would urge everyone to put out any unexpected ideas that come to their mind no matter how silly they may have sounded. That will simulate their heads as they bring up every idea they could have and it would make things seem more interesting as we can talk about any super silly ideas we may have. The third meeting would be focused on choosing three possible solutions we thought were the best and talking about the positives and negatives. In this situation, the solutions would be focused on the main problem, which is funds shortage. Meaning fundraising events would be the best way to roll. The three types of fundraisers would be a car wash trivia night or a community auction. The car wash would be simple to do but I am not sure if it would generate enough cash. The trivia night sounds fun, but we would need to see if the community would be interested. Ultimately, the community auction has the potential to make the most money, but we need to do a bunch of planning which would require us to spend the most amount of money. We would construct a break-even tool for all three of these resolutions to see how much money we would require to put into it and how much money would we need to make to break the event to fund the event. The next meeting would be focused on choosing the best answers out of the three. We would create the rule that everyone had to agree with the idea we were doing to prevent any sort of confrontation. I would suggest we do a combination of a trivia night and a community auction. It would generate a lot of interest in the community and have the potential to bring in a lot of money. If we all chose to go with my idea, we would go into the next meeting getting ready to execute the plan. I would split the group into two different groups. The first group would work towards creating a trivia night. The last group would work towards a community auction. I would split the group according to their SWOT as we are familiar with each other's strengths and weaknesses.

Being in a group as the leader can be difficult. You have to work with group members that you have never met and come to an agreement on a decision without any sort of battle. That's why it is important to use decision tools and a framework. A framework like the P-MOPS will improve your chances of making the best decision with your group. Decision tools will make certain aspects of the group easier like getting to know them or making a decision

Footnote:

Groups are vital in life. Even though I didn't have a lot of family and friends when I came to the United States of America, I had my older brother and a few cousins that I could rely on. They lived near but I could trust in case of an emergency. I wasn't completely alone in my journey.

APPENDIX B

Introduction.

    I will team up with the HR department in order to design a powerful long-term training strategy to embrace a global approach and feedback that can validate employee experience. A good training program for new employees should be focused on precise step-by-step development. I would make sure that the training meets the organization's objective and the employee's motion.

Identify reasons and purpose for conducting employee orientation.

    There are several reasons why orientation is extremely important to jobs. Many new employees are extremely nervous when it comes to their first day at work. Orientation helps ease these employees' nerves as they will not be working the traditional workday. Another great thing about orientation is it gets employees more work-ready. It gives them a preview of what the jobs are like and allows them to connect with their future coworkers. Lastly, it gives employers a chance to see their skills. Since another employee will be in charge of showing new employees around, he will see a couple of things. First, he will see what kind of skills the employee has and how well will he be able to handle the job. Once they figure out this, they can plan how to use the new employee.

Outline what would be covered in the orientation, including the topics and at least ten (10) items prioritized.

The topics covered in the orientation would include: dealing with customers; different types of customers; our products; how the robot works; frequently asked questions; common issues; how to train customers; how to contact technical support, customer follow-up; dealing with unsatisfied customers.

Plan the length of the program, who will conduct it, and what formats will be used.

Because orientation is extremely important, it is vital to make sure you have the best orientation program to prepare new employees. The first thing my orientation would include would be an hour-long talk session with the other employees. It is extremely important to be comfortable with your coworkers, almost as important as the job itself. This will allow the new employee to get more comfortable with the job. Next, I would spend the majority of the orientation talking about the job. I will be telling them things like their job responsibilities, the skills needed for work, and how their day will look. If any questions are asked, the question should be answered as thoroughly as possible to make sure the new employee understands. Next, I would spend the next hour showing him his other coworkers doing their job. I would explain what they are doing, why they are doing it, and how they are doing it. Lastly, I would show the new employee around the building making sure he gets familiarized with it. I would make sure I trained someone to conduct orientations and add an experienced employee. That way, they could answer any questions the new employee may have about the job. That way, they could answer any questions the new employee may have about the job. Orientation would be divided up into two days to prevent giving the new employee too much information at once. The orientation would be offered in two ways: in-person or online.

Describe if and how you would incorporate a web-based component into the program.

We discussed in-person, but online would be handled a little differently. Online would be more information-based because it would be difficult to introduce employees from a webcam/zoom. I would divide the online orientation into different sections and pack as much information as possible for it. I would include everything I discussed for the in-person orientation. I would even include a fun tour of the building and make it interactive so it doesn't get too boring for the new employee.

Summary.

The orientation training will pinpoint any gaps in the new training development and employee skill sets. These gaps should be inspected, arranged, and turned into the organization's training objectives. The main focus is to pinpoint the gap between current and desired performance through the evolution of a training program that has business goals at its origin.

In this scenario, there is a problem between the production manager James and the production employee Maria. The complication started in last week's meeting. Maria told James that there were some production issues their vendor acrylics are changing and that lowers the quality of each good. James asked if anyone else was having the same problem. No one answered James. For that reason, he decided to ignore the warning and called a meeting. One week later, he told the production team that issues like this need to be reported to the manager. Someone may get fired for this. In this instance, I believe very firmly that it's James' fault. He needed to do a much better job as a manager. He did not listen to either one of his employee's warnings as the situation led to major issues throughout the company. Not only that he didn't take responsibility for his actions, he also blamed the production team for his wrongdoing. By contrast, I agree with him that Maria should have written a memo but she did inform him of the issue. Maria should not be fired over this. Based on this situation, James could be seen as an autocratic leader. According to the book, an autocratic leader is an individual who wants the employees to follow his every word as no question asked. Maria did not write a memo, which James stated that she was supposed to do. James was thinking of firing Maria over that situation. I believe that two critical things need to be done about this company.

The first thing that needs to take place is that James needs to get fired or demoted. As a leader, he didn't do a great job. After the meeting, James should have asked Maria to stay a bit to get a bigger picture of what was happening. Second, he should have done his research to discover what created the issue then tried to resolve it. He did not do any of those things. As a result, the company paid the price, and James blamed other people for it. I would fire James and look for a different type of leader. Based on the textbook (Robbins and Judge, 2019), a transformational leader would have prevented this situation from happening. Transformational leaders are seen as a mentor to other employees. They provide clear solutions to different kinds of situations based on information from the book. Hiring this type of leader prevents a situation like this from happening again. Another thing I would do for this company is improve the communication process. Eventually, James was not wrong about everything he was right about the memo aspect. With this kind of issue, I agree that a memo should have been written and sent to all the employees including higher-ups. The communication process should have involved the three parties: sender, channel, and receiver according to the textbook (Robbins and Judge, 2019). The sender puts on a message through a channel. The receiver takes that message and sends back feedback through the channel. For example, Maria could have been the sender, and James the receiver. That situation occurred because there was no channel between them, and the company had to create one.

For this company, I believe that emailing would be the best channel for all parties. It would create proof that messages were sent and prevent people from forgetting important information. Also, emailing would create a better relationship throughout the workplace. Managers and high-ups could use emails to keep up with how employees are doing and this could create better relationships among everyone. Maybe a weekly email asking people how their weeks are and if they have any plans for the weekend. This email would promote a healthy relationship for everyone. The leader could also use emails to keep himself updated with potential problems. He could have a weekly check-up asking if there are any new problems with the products. This would keep him involved and prevent major issues from piling up.

It can hurt a company or an organization when negative office politics start to occur in the workplace. Office politics can tear the place apart by dividing teammates, supervisors, and managers which in the long run can turn the place upside down. Moreover, it can cut back on productivity, and employee morale. If office politics are left unresolved it can damage the reputation of the organization or the company.

One example would be a power struggle between a male and a female manager at my old job. The two managers were competing for an open position and got everyone in the office involved. They were exchanging words, and the guy called the female manager ugly, stupid and uneducated. I observed the whole argument and I thought that everything was blown out of proportion. Upper management got involved and called me as a witness. I was not sure what to do because I have a good relationship with both managers.

Finally, as much as I hate to be part of the bandwagon fallacy they are left with no choice other than to tell the truth.

Footnote:

The first thing I learned in America is that power is essential and can influence people's conception of you positively. At first, I had no control over anything, even how my life was going to unfold. Therefore, my skills were poor as I was learning the facts of life. I was just a rookie in all aspects of my life. My English was not great plus I had a small amount of money in my pocket. Few weeks later I bumped into a longtime friend of mine who happened to live not too far from where I was staying. He kindly offered me a place to stay. At first, things were great as he was very understanding of my situation, however, he began to treat me more like a tenant rather than a friend. I didn't like the way he was treating me though, we broke apart as I went to get my own place to live. I feel like I gained power over my life and things started to fall into place.

According to the textbook, POLC stands for the four functions of management, which are planning, organizing, leading, and controlling. Planning is the function I probably use the most as it is important to my personal life. My day will change drastically if I don't plan it out, so I like to make plans the day before. Organizing and leading are more useful for my work life as I do these functions very often. I will set up an event for work by gathering the right people for the job and will direct people to prevent any problems.

These two functions are very important for my work life and are vital for anyone who wants to have a high position in a company. Controlling is the function I use the least as I do not evaluate how well of a job coworkers are doing. Controlling is mostly used for my personal life towards my kids as I will let them know if they are on the right track or not.

If I had to grade myself on my strongest plus weakest function, it would be planning my best and controlling my worst. This is because I am planning everything throughout the day, learning from my previous mistakes. Because controlling is the one I use the least, I do not get the chance to learn from my mistakes. If I used it more, I have no doubt my skills in controlling would improve.

The chief financial officer (CFOs) holds the top financial position in an organization. They are responsible for tracking cash flow and financial planning and analyzing the company's financial strengths and weaknesses and proposing strategic directions.

A CFO is in charge of a company's financial operations. This includes responsibility for internal and external financial reporting, stewardship of a company's assets, and ownership of cash management. Increasingly, the role is more forward-looking and expanding to incorporate strategy and business partnership.

Ethics in finance demands adherence to the highest standards. The consequences of unethical behavior are clear, from loss of reputation and trust to monetary penalty and criminal prosecution. Effective leaders attend to an inner moral compass which helps minimize the temptation toward unethical behavior.

The importance of ethics in finance is well understood, at least in a general sense. Often, however, ethics are practiced in a rote, nonreflective way. Business leaders in the financial sector must move beyond simple compliance and rule-based consideration. Ethics in finance demands adherence to the highest standards.

The consequences of unethical behavior are clear, from loss of reputation and trust to monetary penalty and criminal prosecution. Effective leaders attend to an inner moral compass which helps minimize the temptation toward unethical behavior.

Still, good people make bad decisions. Ethical leadership goes beyond good intentions and knowing the rules. The pressures of a fast-moving, complex marketplace can lead us into reactive decision-making and possibly unethical behavior. Without a planned framework of integrity at the core of any business decision, ethics risk compromise.

Footnote:
To my way of thinking, when the going gets tough, people have a tendency to act unethically. No matter how difficult life is, nobody should ever think that way. Even when I was struggling I didn't do any questionable stuff!

Investing is particularly essential when it comes to making money. Accomplishing it wisely can transform your life for good. When you invest carelessly it can have harmful effects on the investor. That's why it is essential to make sure you glance at all the probable curves of an investment. For instance, we will be examining an investment option that could make us a lot of money. In that instance, we are an investor in Angel, and we are operating with an entrepreneur as debt financing will usually concern two parties but there can be others as well.

By investing money conservatively someone could profit greatly from it as opposed to doing it poorly. Investing money wisely can transform your life permanently. When investing, it is important to evaluate all the imaginable slopes of an investment. For instance, we will look at an investment option that could make us a lot of cash. In that instance, we are an investor in Angel, and we are working with an entrepreneur as debt financing usually concerns two parties, though there can be more. It is an agreement between two or more parties that states one party will supply the other with the capital in exchange for paying back the money with interest. There are several benefits to debt financing such as earning money that you didn't once have and you will keep the rights of your business, unlike equity financing. Thus, one of the biggest benefits of debt financing is the tax advantages. With debt financing, the more money that is provided to you, the more interest you will have to pay on it. When paying interest, the money is gone, and there is no benefit to yourself. Despite all, with debt financing, all interest paid will be tax deductible. That is almost one negative aspect of interest and can be seen as an encouragement to borrow as much money as you can pay off as the interesting aspect will do very little harm to your business.

To calculate the AT-WACC, there will be various numbers that we need to plug in. When we insert the numbers into the formula it looks like this:

$$\text{AT-WACC} = 10\% \times (1-0.32) \times 0.5 + 14\% \times 0.5$$

When we go through this formula, the answer that we come up with is 10.4%. AT-WACC is 10% with the 50/50 equity financing structure. According to the information we were provided, the return on investment is 9%. The Weighted Average Cost of Capital represents how much capital a business will have after all its expenses and revenue come together. For example, if a business makes around 1 million dollars in sales, the Weighted Average Cost of Capital would come down to 100,000 dollars. The return on investment is less than the AT-WACC, meaning that I would be losing about 1%

of my investment. Indeed, that investment would not make a lot of sense to me as it would only help me lose money steadily.

If I am looking to make money for an investment, I would need to find an investment that makes more than 10.4%. The only way this investment would work is if we increase the debt amount of our AT-WACC. If we increase the debt aspect of the AT-WACC, it would increase our return on investment enough to turn this into a positive investment.

Unified Commercial Code-1 or the UCC-1 is defined as a document that creditors used to let the other party know the right to seize their assets. In this example, we are an investor who is putting money into Angel. Because you are investing in Angel, you are protected from any negative impact if you are using more debt if the company goes bankrupt, according to the UCC-1. That means when you are investing with Angel, we should make sure we are using debt so that in case the business fails, we will pursue our right to claim their assets.

This example showcases why investing wisely is extremely important. If we would blindly give up our money to this investment, we would make slightly less money than when we put in, which would slowly bleed our money for even more losses. When we were able to crunch the numbers and change certain aspects of our investment, we were able to figure out a way to make money!

One party will supply the other party with money in exchange for paying back with interest. There are various advantages to debt financing such as getting capital we didn't have previously, and we will keep ownership of the business, unlike equity financing. One of the major advantages of debt financing is the tax benefits. With debt financing, the more money that is provided to you, the more interest you will have to pay on it. After all, when you are paying interest, the money's gone and there is no benefit to yourself. Despite all, with debt financing, all interest paid will be tax deductible. This almost negates the negative aspect of interest and can be seen as an encouragement to borrow as much money as you can pay off as the interesting aspect will do very little harm to your business.

Footnote:

Investing is a very important part of anyone's life. I wished that I had tackled that one aspect way sooner. Lately, I have been doing a lot of investments for my friends and family as they're very happy about the returns they're getting on their investments. Day and day out I tell my children to learn from the mistakes that I made in my youth. The good investment that you make today is going to determine how the rest of your life is going to be. Therefore, pay attention, listen, and learn from your parents. I guarantee that you will benefit tremendously from that one aspect alone.

From an outstanding point of view, a good employee is someone who can contribute a lot to the success of an organization. It is also an employee that understands his/her role therefore, he/she will keep his attitude intact for the prosperity of the business. Let us take a look at these employees to see if the employees are compliant with their organization.

Employee #1: Employee #1 feels distant when her boss tells her she should not worry about the lower end of the market. "Those people don't have much buying power." She was offended. She felt like she was being attacked, too, because her family is from the lower end of the market. After all, the company's values statement says that the company values the welfare of everyone. The reason why she has a negative attitude toward her boss is the fact that she is also from a blue-collar family. They don't have a lot of money to spend on goods and services. Therefore, as a manager, she should not worry much about them. The company can't prosper with them. Perhaps she felt that her blue-collar group was not well represented by this company. It is a double standard and it is hard to follow if you're trying to do the right thing. As far as being late for work I blamed her for that. Whether you disliked or didn't like your supervisor at work it is not a valid reason for being late all the time. She could have tried to talk to her boss about any personal or work-related issues to resolve the problem. This kind of behavior is only going to hurt the organization in the end. In this situation, I would strictly talk to her supervisor. I would let him know this type of behavior is not acceptable. He would not comply, there would be consequences such as termination from the company. I would also pull Employee #1 to the side and apologize for her boss's behavior. I would let her know that this type of attitude is not normal and this would not happen again. According to Mintzberg, I would be acting like Liaison. I solved the conflict between the boss and Employee #1.

Employee #2: Staff #2 loves the work and he loves the job. However, the long hours are killing him by stressing him out. Despite him being loyal to the company, the stress is forcing him to look for another job. As an engineer, he is very valuable to the company. Indeed, stress could have serious consequences. One problem that stress creates is that it can lead to health problems. Based on information from an article (Maulik, 2017), some of these problems include hypertension and cardiovascular disease. These problems can lead to losing Employee #2 indefinitely. Also, if he is stressed out he will not think clearly. This could lead to mistakes that can hurt the company financially. One solution the manager should take is to hire another engineer. This will cut on his hours and create less work for him. According to Mintzberg, I would be acting like a resource allocator. I would decide by hiring a new staff, which would fall under the resource allocator.

Employee #3: Staff #3 is not happy about the job. She complains about the offices and working conditions to other staff. Her complaints harm the other employees. As a result, the shift she works has lower productivity than normal. This is bad for the company for several reasons. First, it lowers the other staff's morale. This can have an impact on the effort and culture of the workplace. Also if the productivity is lower than normal, the company will be losing money. This could also be bad for employee turnover. If the staff are not happy, they will quit and look for other jobs. The solution would be to confront Employee #3 about her issues with the company. We would ask her and everyone on the shift what the issues are and what we can do to resolve the problems. Once we get feedback, we would implement these changes as soon as possible. According to

Mintzberg, I would be acting as a disturbance handler and a monitor. The company has a problem with their employees in this shift regarding the work conditions. I would be getting information just to handle any obstacles that come my way. With the capability to collect information and solve issues that are combined with emotions seems like I am equipped to handle any situations that come my way.

Employee #4: Employee #4 feels like the company's values are not being respected. The company is not diverse, therefore, he doesn't feel included. However, Employee #4 is because he is the only Hispanic working there, and he is a placeholder for the job. Based on information from an article (Henry Inegbedion, 2020), not being diverse leads to many problems for the company. Moreover, a lack of diversity limits your market as people from other cultures would feel uncomfortable buying your products. This will lead to a loss of profit for the company. Also, this will create a hostile working environment. This will be bad for employee morale and will create problems such as high employee turnover, and decreased productivity. For a solution, I would change our hiring practices. I would try to find candidates that fit the needs of the company while looking for diverse people with different mindsets. Also, I would offer Employee #4 a permanent position as he feels strongly about the company's values. This shows me that he cares about the company and would make an excellent addition to it. According to Mintzberg, I would be acting as a leader and a liaison. I would be changing my entire organization set up and the networking behind it. These two things fall into both categories of leader and liaison.

Finally, I concluded that every single one of those employees has their particular problem. After all, it's up to the company to accommodate their employees, and for the employees to work their best to satisfy the employers.

Footnote:

Having a good relationship with your coworkers is huge especially if you plan on staying at that job. A bad relationship with coworkers will cause problems that can easily be avoided. Some of the closest people I met have come from a previous workplace, so it's important to be friendly at work.

Resources:

Maulik, P. K. (2017, October 1). Workplace stress: A neglected aspect of mental health wellbeing. The Indian journal of medical research. Retrieved January 18, 2022, from https://www.ncbi.nlm.nih.gov/pmc/articles/PMC5819024/

Henry Inegbedion, E. S. (2020, January 10). Managing diversity for organizational efficiency—Henry Inegbedion, eze Sunday, Abiola Asaleye, Adedoyin Lawal, Ayeni Adebanji, 2020. SAGE Journals. Retrieved January 18, 2022, from https://journals.sagepub.com/doi/10.1177/2158244019900173

APPENDIX C

For this assignment, the company I will be using is Netflix. The business process will be improving its subscription service. The two stakeholders in this process will be the subscribers to Netflix as customers and shareholders. Both of these groups of people will love to see the substitution process improve for different reasons. Many customers have left Netflix because of how clunky their subscription service works; which affects the amount of revenue that is coming up (shareholders). The customers will expect this project to improve the smoothness/features of the substitution service. And shareholders expect this project to increase the number of people who join the service.

This project will improve how people can buy subscriptions for their family and friends. That is the number one complaint from customers, therefore, we hope we can get rid of that with this project. We also want more people to join our service. We could increase the amount of revenue for our shareholders. There are two major things we will be adding: a referral program and reverting how many people can use a subscription. One of the most controversial things that have changed with Netflix is the number of people that are able to use a subscription. Many people were upset with how many people were allowed to use an account, though we will be switching back to our old model.

This will make the customers happy, and regain our lost subscribers. We will increase the revenue for our shareholders. Additionally, we will introduce a referral program that will get customers a free 15 days of Netflix if they refer their friends. This will add an incentive to customers to share this service with their friends, which will increase our sub count. We will be tracking the results of these changes in two ways.

First, we will compare the number of subscribers we gained with the average amount we encounter. Second, we will send out a bi-monthly survey asking how much the customers like our substitution services and changes. With these changes, I hope people will be happier with our subscription services, which will attract more customers and drive up the stock price for our shareholders.

Human Resource management tasks are not as easy as many of us would think/imagine. After all, we're humans and we make decisions at times beyond comprehension especially under pressure. All Souls Hospital was pretty busy that week and two incidents occurred. First, one employee who was a future union representative got fired for using the company's computer to talk to other employees about the union's movement. Lastly, a veteran applied for a position in which she did not get hired. At last, she accused management of foul play.

The First scenario of the employee that recently got fired was about 24 hours away from being a union representative. The employer confirmed their decision by attesting that they observed her going on social media talking at lunchtime to other employees about union-related problems on the company's computers. The former employee filed a complaint with the Regional Office usually with the guidance of the report Officer.

This particular employee is supported under the NLRA law. The NLRA is a federal law that enables employees the right to participate in union activities. Additionally to enroll in protected and agreed-upon movements that help working conditions. It also protects them from renouncing union movements. (NLRB, N.D.) The Labor Relations Board emphasizes this act. This law, after all, doesn't look after government employees, individuals who work in agriculture, or self-supporting contractors or supervisors. At last, if an employee senses that his/her freedom has been disturbed he/she must file an accusation with their regional offices.

One law relating to this case would be the Health Insurance Portability and Accountability Act. According to the CDC, the Health Insurance Portability and Accountability Act is a "federal law that requires the creation of national standards to protect sensitive patient health information from being disclosed without the patient's consent or knowledge." Because the employee was talking with other employees in a public setting about important job-related topics, it can be viewed that they handed out important medical information which would be a breach of Hippa.

For the female veteran case, one important detail is that she served in the military. The Uniformed Services Employment and Reemployment Rights Act is defined by the O.S.C as "a federal law, passed in 1994, that protects military service members and veterans from employment discrimination based on their service, and allows them to regain their civilian jobs following a period of uniformed service." This act states that employers cannot refuse to hire someone because they served in the military. The Equal Credit Opportunity Act of 1974 also plays a role here. This act stipulates that everyone must be given a fair chance, and cannot be discriminated against based on things like sex and color. At last, the female veteran can dispute that she wasn't given a fair opportunity because she was a woman.

The National Labor Relation Board or NLRB, has a series of steps to follow when they hear of potential cases like these. First, they listen up to the charges that the case is being built upon, such as harassment charges by the female veteran. Second of all, they conduct an investigation. Finally, the NLRB would look into things and come up with a conclusion or solution. And the question to ask in this situation is: as a future union representative what was she saying online to other employees at lunchtime? Especially when she was using the company's computer during her lunchtime. After all, the NLRB would hold a hearing where they would listen to both sides and then proceed with all the information they gathered.

The Equal Employment Opportunity Commission or EEOC is a federal agency that creates laws to protect people in the workplace. For the female veteran case, many laws passed by the EEOC would be brought up. The Civil Rights Act of 1964 would be involved because she can argue that she wasn't hired because of her sex. The Equal Pay Act of 1963 is relative to this case because it would prevent the employer from punishing the female veteran for this charge. The

Civil Rights Act of 1991 would be important as it allows jury trials to give employees like her things like money damages. The Pregnancy Discrimination Act may be used as well as it might be important depending on the age of the female veteran.

Based on the two incidents that happened at the hospital human resources personnel would need to be extra careful next time to avoid similar problems. In the veteran case, perhaps they could have chosen multiple interviewers of both sexes to conduct the interview. Indeed, that would have made the interviewee feel more comfortable and prevent a harassment case. Moreover, they could have sent a letter or emailed the interviewees to let them know why they were not hired. For the union representative case, one major thing they could have done is make a social media policy. Let employees know beforehand that talking about the company's information online will not be authorized and make sure to include it in employee handbooks. Also, they should make an effort to brace the union as it would avoid problems like this from arising next.

APPENDIX D

Time plays an essential concept in many different circumstances. One aspect of time plays a huge role is money. The time value of money calculates how much money is being made during a specific portion of time. The time value of money is important for assets because it shows individuals a good sense of how their investments are performing. You can even use the time value of money in different investments to see which investment will make the most money in different time frames. In this instance, we will be examining the time value of money and calculating it to see if the investment we were looking at is right or not.

To calculate the time value of money, there will be something that we will need to know. The net present value will be a big aspect of calculating cash flow and will let us know certain aspects of the time value of money. According to Investopedia, Present value is "the difference between the present value of cash inflows and the present value of cash outflows over a period of time." This is important because the net present value can tell us how profitable an investment is; which will save us a lot of time when figuring out if certain investments are worth our time. The formula for net present value is net present value = future value/(1+ discount rate)^year of cash flow. With the formula at hand, we can calculate the discounted cash flow in year 4 which is stated to be less than 30,000. 30,0000 is our future value, the year will be 4 and the discount rate will be 13%. Now that we have all of these numbers, we can plug them into our net present value formula.

Present value=30,000/(1+.13)^4=18399.5618304-> 18399.56

For the net present value, we would have to look at each different cash flow and discount them.

NPV=-90,0000+30,000/(1+.13)+30,000/(1+.13)^2+30,000/(1+.13)^3+30,000/(1+.13)^4=-765.860233702-> -765.86

The net present value would be negative, which would signal that the investment would be losing money over time. Therefore, the investment opportunity should not be accepted.

Now just because this investment is not good doesn't mean all similar investments will play out the same way. For example, we will look at a similar example besides a few exceptions. We will change the discount rate from 13% to 8% to see if that changes the investment.

NPV=-90,0000+30,000/(1+.08)+30,000/(1+.08)^2+30,000/(1+.08)^3+30,000/(1+.08)^4=9363.8052013->9363.81

This would be a positive NPV, meaning the investment would be making money over time. Therefore, I would accept this project. Just changing a few factors of our investment would change the amount of money for the project significantly. That's why it is important to look at each investment opportunity very thoroughly as small details can yield much better or worse results.

The time value of money is extremely important for any investment. It shows you how much your money can be worth depending on what investment you will choose. Investing is a hard thing to do, especially if you are trying to make the most amount of money possible. That's why when investing, remembering the time value of money can be the difference between a successful investment and a bad one.

Footnote:

Time management is a crucial skill that everyone must learn about if you want to move ahead in life. I wasted a lot of time in my youth by not following my dreams to achieve my goals. Nowadays, I am using time management to the best of my ability and I teach the importance of it to my children.

Reference:

Parrino, R., Kidwell, D. S., Bates, T., & Gillan, S. L. (2021). Fundamentals of Corporate Finance, Enhanced eText (5th ed.). Wiley Global Education US.

Fernando, J. (2022, November 16). Net present value (NPV): What it means and steps to calculate it. Investopedia. Retrieved January 17, 2023, from https://www.investopedia.com/terms/n/npv.asp#:~:text=Net%20present%20value%20(NPV)%20is,a%20projected%20investment%20or%20project.

APPENDIX E

By investing money conservatively someone could profit greatly from it as opposed to doing it poorly. Investing money wisely can transform your life permanently. When investing, it is important to evaluate all the imaginable slopes of an investment. For instance, we will look at an investment option that could make us a lot of cash. In that instance, we are an investor in Angel, and we are working with an entrepreneur as debt financing usually concerns two parties, though there can be more. It is an agreement between two or more parties that states one party will supply the other with the capital in exchange for paying back the money with interest. There are several benefits to debt financing such as earning money that you didn't once have and you will keep the rights of your business, unlike equity financing. Thus, one of the biggest benefits of debt financing is the tax advantages. With debt financing the more money that is provided to you the more interest, you will have to pay on it. When paying interest, the money is gone, and there is no benefit to yourself. Despite all, with debt financing, all interest paid will be tax deductible. That is almost one negative aspect of interest and can be seen as an encourager to borrow as much money as you can pay off as the interesting aspect will do very little harm to your business.

To calculate the AT-WACC, there will be various numbers that we need to plug in. When we insert the numbers into the formula it looks like this:

$$\text{AT-WACC} = 10\% \times (1-0.32) \times 0.5 + 14\% \times 0.5$$

When we go through this formula, the answer that we come up with is 10.4%. AT-WACC is 10% with the 50/50 equity financing structure. According to the information we were provided, the return on investment is 9%. The Weighted Average Cost of Capital represents how much capital a business will have after all its expenses and revenue come together. For example, if a business makes around 1 million dollars in sales, the Weighted Average Cost of Capital would come down to 100,000 dollars. The return on investment is less than the AT-WACC, meaning that I would be losing about 1% of my investment. Indeed, that investment would not make a lot of sense to me as it would only help me lose money steadily.

If I am looking to make money for an investment, I would need to find an investment that makes more than 10.4%. The only way this investment would work is if we increase the debt amount of our AT-WACC. If we increase the debt aspect of the AT-WACC, it would increase our return on investment enough to turn this into a positive investment.

Unified Commercial Code-1 or the UCC-1 is defined as a document that creditors used to let the other party know the right to seize their assets. In this example, we are an investor who is putting money into Angel. Because you are investing in Angel, you are protected from any negative impact if you are using more debt if the company goes bankrupt, according to the UCC-1. That means when you are investing with Angel, we should make sure we are using debt so that in case the business fails, we will pursue our right to claim their assets.

This example showcases why investing wisely is extremely important. If we would blindly give up our money to this investment, we would make slightly less money than when we put in, which would slowly bleed our money for even more losses. When we were able to crunch the numbers and change certain aspects of our investment, we were able to figure out a way to make money!

One party will supply the other party with money in exchange for paying back with interest. There are various advantages to debt financing such as getting capital we didn't have previously, and we will keep ownership of the business, unlike equity financing. One of the major advantages of debt financing is the tax benefits. With debt financing, the more money that is provided to you, the more interest you will have to pay on it. After all, when you are paying interest, the money's gone and there is no benefit to yourself. Despite all, with debt financing, all interest paid will be tax deductible. This almost negates the negative aspect of interest and can be seen as an encouragement to borrow as much money as you can pay off as the interesting aspect will do very little harm to your business.

Note:
The concept of debt has been confusing to me and as I have progressed through life, I have a better understanding of it. When I was younger, I hated the thought of being in debt. If I owed any money at all, I would make sure to pay all of it back; even if it meant I was going to use up every last penny. Now, I understand that not all debt is bad and how to manage debt to risk regarding my bills and investments.

Reference:
Parrino, R., Kidwell, D. S., Bates, T., & Gillan, S. L. (2021). Fundamentals of Corporate Finance, Enhanced eText (5th ed.). Wiley Global Education US.

ARDITTI, F. D. (1973). The Weighted Average Cost of Capital: Some Questions on Its Definition, Interpretation, and Use. Journal of Finance (Wiley-Blackwell), 28(4), 1001–1007. https://doi-org.libauth.purdueglobal.edu/10.1111/j.1540-6261.1973.tb01422.x

Deuis kartinah, Dicky Jhoansyah, & Faizal Mulia Z. (2021). Analyze Return on Equity and Weighted Average Cost of Capital Linkages to Firm Value. Almana: Jurnal Manajemen Dan Bisnis, 5(1). https://doi-org.libauth.purdueglobal.edu/10.36555/almana.v5i1.1411

APPENDIX F

As defined in the book, "Decisions such as whom to hire, what to pay, what training to offer, and how to evaluate employee performance directly affect employees' motivation and ability to provide goods and services that customers value. Companies that attempt to increase their competitiveness by investing in new technology and promoting quality throughout the organization also invest in state-of-the-art staffing, training, and compensation practices."

Basically managing human resources attributes to the role that a manager fulfills parallel to the organization's employees. Managing Human Resources can relate to the act of delivering the management including planning and allocating resources. For example, hiring the right candidates for the job or providing good benefits to motivate other employees to work or join the organization.

Human resources can be a changing factor for a business. A good example of this would be Apple's success as a business. In the early 2000s, Apple was not successful. For that, the company was in search of a new CEO to change the course of the company. Eventually, human resources would look back and hire one of their previous CEOs, Steve Jobs. By rehiring Steve Jobs he would take Apple from a mid-tier company to one of the biggest in the world.

Finally, human resources functions are not just hiring and firing employees. It can be many things such as providing benefits, motivating employees, or hiring the right candidates for certain positions. Most definitely, human resource management plays an important role in a company's success.

While on the subject of HRM here is a very delicate one that is causing a major problem for HR personnel in an organization. It is when robots are making decisions for humans. For example read this below:

Robotic Willy

From an understanding point of view it's a huge problem for a company when robots make human decisions or replace manpower. If programmed right robots can be extremely intelligent and more but, we must be conscious about one thing. They're not human, they have no sensibility, no compassion and most certainly, they're not human. They're machines.

Answer: The company's hiring practices have a major issue. The hiring system is too focused on technology and automation, and there is very little involvement of actual HR executives. That can be a problem because the automated system may not grasp the importance of diversity and minorities in the hiring process.

Human Resource Management is a wide subject including many topics, elements and basic concepts of how the most important asset of an organization should be well managed effectively and efficiently so as to achieve the organization's goal. The problem…

Assignment: Needed Diversity at MTE

Introduction: You read about and practiced with some concepts related to equal employment opportunity in the workplace in the Learning Activity. Now you will apply some of these concepts to a scenario. Read the following scenario and respond in a business memo to the checklist items.

Scenario: MTE is a robotics firm that has clients all over the world but is based in the US., with offices in most major cities. Recently MTE has been experiencing an upsurge in indiscrimination lawsuits by women and minorities since they grew from 2,000 employees in 2016 to have 3,500 employees by the third quarter of 2019. A demand for their technology services exploded with the expansion of some of their clients' high-technology needs in the medical industry. There are currently 3,000 employees in the Northeastern US., and 500 employees in other countries. The lawsuits claim that women and minorities are not being hired in equitable numbers due to a discriminatory hiring system. MTE has an automated hiring system in place on its hiring website. According to the process, applicants must first submit their resumes, which are scanned for specific educational requirements such as top 10 university degrees and key phrases. After this initial scan, the system likely filters out applicants who do not meet the specified criteria

Discrimination in the workplace, either overt or subtle, can greatly harm employees' work experiences as well as expose the company to litigation if it violates any of the federal or state laws in place to protect certain groups. Discrimination against members of any minority group, whether based on race, color or other classification, occurs when members of such a group are treated differently from other employees, solely because they are among that group.

Minority discrimination can exist even in a company with a diverse workforce that includes a number of Asian, Hispanic and African Americans. The term "glass ceiling" often refers to female employees who are not able to advance beyond certain title and pay levels, but the term also applies to others who are members of ethnic minorities. They may find that they don't receive the same pay as their other counterparts, or they are passed over for promotion in favor of other candidates despite equal qualifications.

APPENDIX G

Human Resource Management
Memo
To: MTE
From: Willy V
Date: October 21st, 2021
Re: Needed Diversity at MTE

    The purpose of my memo is to express my concern about the hiring process and the lack of diversification that exists at MTE. To my understanding, the company's human resource department is filled with robots instead of human beings as employees. I would understand if these robots were in charge of doing manual labor, but the human resources would be too advanced for a robot to handle. Human resources are one of the most important aspects of a business and they are important for many things. For example, Human resource's biggest responsibility is hiring the right candidates for the company. How are robots able to judge which candidates are right for the company without things like emotions? The robots would not be able to find which candidates are good fits and would be choosing people almost randomly.

    First of all, human resource roles or responsibilities are too important to leave in the robot's hands. Therefore, maintaining a positive workplace culture in the company would be extremely difficult. Human resources are constantly doing little things to make sure employees' morale, listening to their issues in the workplace, and solving internal problems inside the company are in good order. Robots lack empathy, they can only program to work, they cannot think as human beings. Respectfully they would ignore all the personal issues that we are facing at work. Indeed, it would be very difficult for the company to move forward financially. Under circumstances, the company would be a terrible environment to work in. Afterward, MTE has broken the Equal Employment Opportunity Act of 1972 because of the robot screening process. This law states that employers cannot discriminate based on a person's race. The robots do not know this and have probably skipped over many minorities; which could be considered giving them an unequal opportunity.

If we were to replace robots with humans we would be able to hire a diverse set of employees. They would bring different viewpoints and problem-solving skills to the company. For example, in my previous job, I was in a group filled with different types of people. There was a serious problem with a computer virus that no one in the company could figure out and it could have cost the business millions of dollars. A newly hired female had figured out what was wrong and was able to save the business from losing money. Now, imagine what would have happened with robots being in charge of the hiring process. My company would have passed on a candidate like her. Things like these are small examples of why it's important to have different types of people working in the same company and show how hiring one employee can be very important.

Let us skip the subject of HRM for a moment and focus our undivided attention on how important it is for anyone to understand the importance of communication all across the board. When it comes to communication, it's like a universal key that can unlock any type of door. The same thing goes for a wonderful and successful relationship whether it's with a professional, friends, family, or business. We need communication on our corner. Without effective communication, we certainly are not going anywhere. Nowadays we depend on the internet, and digital communication skills are really necessary to get messages across. In the meantime, we must make things as clear as possible in order to avoid confusion.

As we all know, some forms of online communication don't permit right away feedback. Therefore, it is important to pass messages in specific settings just to be safe.

Some forms of online communication do not allow immediate feedback, so it's essential to present messages in a one-way setting in order to be at the top of the game. Communication failures, on the other hand, are very critical and the price to pay can be hurtful. When customers don't grasp your messages very well they draw terrible conclusions about your brand.

The article I used is "The Importance of Great Communication Skills in Business."

Some forms of online communication do not allow immediate feedback, so it's essential to present compelling messages in a one-way setting in order to be successful. Communication failures, on the other hand, come at no small price—when customers receive poorly crafted messages, they form unfavorable conclusions about your brand.

As we all know, there aren't many chances to improve the first impression. These five useful skills for online communication will help you avoid unnecessary complications and improve the profitability of your business. Let's see what you should consider.

1. Follow "netiquette"

When people meet in person for the first time, there are certain unwritten rules of it's customary to behave with propriety and decorum. Ignoring these rules risks coming across as rude, arrogant, or just plain odd, creating barriers to constructive dialog as a result and damaging any potential relationships before they've even begun. Well, online communication works in a similar way, with a similar set of standards.

"Netiquette" is the framework of accepted behaviors when communicating online. In many ways, the importance of netiquette exceeds that of in-person etiquette, because unlike fleeting acquaintances, the internet creates a permanent record of communications which can haunt people and businesses that have been ineffective or offensive in previous online interactions. Avoid such communication at all costs; you don't need the Ghost of Bad Online Past hovering above you and ruining your reputation, that's for sure.

This particular instance we're going to acknowledge good employees and how important they are for the success of an organization. From an outstanding point of view, a good employee is someone who can contribute a lot to the success of an organization. It is also, an employee that understands his/her role therefore, he/she will keep his attitude intact for the prosperity of the business. Let us take a look at these employees to see if the employees are compliant with their organization.

Employee #1: Employee #1 feels distant when her boss tells her she should not worry about the lower end of the market. "Those people don't have much buying power." The reason why she has a negative attitude toward her boss is the fact that she is also from a blue-collar family. They don't have a lot of money to spend on goods and services. Therefore, as a manager, she should not worry much about them. The company can't prosper with them. Perhaps she felt that her blue-collar group was not well represented by this company. It is a double standard and it is hard to follow if you're trying to do the right thing. As far as being late for work I blamed her for that. Whether you disliked or didn't like your supervisor at work it is not a valid reason for being late all the time. She could have tried to talk to her boss about any personal or work-related issues to resolve the problem. This kind of behavior is only going to hurt the organization in the end. In this situation, I would strictly talk to her supervisor. I would let him know this type of behavior is not acceptable. He would not comply, there would be consequences such as termination from the company. I would also pull Employee #1 to the side and apologize for her bosses' behavior. I would let her know that this type of attitude is not normal and this would not happen again. According to Mintzberg, I would be acting like Liaison. I solved the conflict between the boss and Employee #1.

Employee #2: Staff #2 loves the work and he loves the job. However, the long hours are killing him by stressing him out. Despite him being loyal to the company, the stress is forcing him to look for another job. As an engineer, he is very valuable to the company.

Therefore, stress could have serious consequences. One problem that stress creates is that it can lead to health problems. Based on information from an article (Maulik, 2017), some of these problems include hypertension and cardiovascular disease. These problems can lead to losing Employee #2 indefinitely. Also, if he is stressed out he will not think clearly. This could lead to mistakes that can hurt the company financially. One solution the manager should take is to hire another engineer. This will cut on his hours and create less work for him. According to Mintzberg, I would be acting like a resource allocator. I would decide by hiring a new staff, which would fall under the resource allocator.

Employee #3: Staff #3 is not happy about the job. She complains about the offices and working conditions to other staff. Her complaints harm the other employees. As a result, the shift she works has lower productivity than normal. This is bad for the company for several reasons. First, it lowers the other staff's morale. This can have an impact on the effort and culture of the workplace. Also if the productivity is lower than normal, the company will be losing money. This could also be bad for employee turnover. If the staff are not happy, they will quit and look for other jobs. The solution would be to confront Employee #3 about her issues with the company. We would ask her and everyone on the shift what the issues are and what we can do to resolve the problems. Once we get feedback, we would implement these changes as soon as possible. According to Mintzberg, I would be acting as a disturbance handler and a monitor. The company has a problem with their employees in this shift regarding the work conditions. I would be getting information and solving the issue, making me a Disturbance Handler (someone who is tasked with making decisions when a company is facing trouble).

Employee #4: Employee #4 feels like the company's values are not being respected. The company is not diverse, therefore, he doesn't feel included. However, Employee #4 is because he is the only Hispanic working there, and he is a placeholder for the job. Based on information from an article (Henry Inegbedion, 2020), not being diverse leads to many problems for the company. Moreover, a lack of diversity limits your market as people from other cultures would feel uncomfortable buying your products. This will lead to a loss of profit for the company. Also, this will create a hostile working environment. This will be bad for employee morale and will create problems such as high employee turnover, and decreased productivity. For a solution, I would change our hiring practices. I would try to find candidates that fit the needs of the company while looking for diverse people with different mindsets. Also, I would offer Employee #4 a permanent position as he feels strongly about the company's values. This shows me that he cares about the company and would make an excellent addition to it. According to Mintzberg, I would be acting as a leader and a liaison. I would be changing my entire organization set up and the networking behind it. These two things fall into both categories of leader and liaison.

Finally, I concluded that every single one of those employees has their particular problem. After all, it's up to the company to accommodate their employees, and for the employees to work their best to satisfy the employers.

Resources:
Maulik, P. K. (2017, October 1). Workplace stress: A neglected aspect of mental health wellbeing. The Indian journal of medical research. Retrieved January 18, 2022, from https://www.ncbi.nlm.nih.gov/pmc/articles/PMC5819024/
Henry Inegbedion, E. S. (2020, January 10). Managing diversity for organizational efficiency—Henry Inegbedion, eze Sunday, Abiola Asaleye, Adedoyin Lawal, Ayeni Adebanji, 2020. SAGE Journals. Retrieved January 18, 2022, from https://journals.sagepub.com/doi/10.1177/2158244019900173

APPENDIX H

"Motivation is a driving force thanks to which an entity undertakes efforts in the hope of achieving its objectives" (Koziol, L., & Koziol, M., 2020). If your employees are not motivated, there will be many consequences. The Timber Building Company is described as a business that builds and modifies offices. Lately, they have had issues that are widespread among the company.

One issue that the company has had is that the CEO and president are thinking of retirement. Another issue with the company is that their engineers are unmotivated and don't work as hard. The supervisor who is in charge of the production line and his technicians have been coming to work late.

This passage of information is from my previous assignment (Willy, 2022). "There are three motivational concepts people tend to focus on. These three are self-efficacy, reinforcement theory, and expectancy theory. According to the book (Robbins and Judge, 2019), the reinforcement theory is the idea that people will do things that lead to positive results and avoid things that bring negative results. In the book (Robbins and Judge 2019), the self-efficacy theory is defined as the ability to use goals to create positive behavior. Lastly, expectancy theory is almost the opposite of self-efficacy as effort will lead to the completion of goals based on information from the book (Robbins and Judge 2019)." These theories are important because they give us reasons why these employees are not motivated. By reviewing these theories, we can see where each employee falls under and find the reason why they are not motivated. For the CEO and president, I think their lack of motivation falls under the self-efficacy theory. They do not have any new goals for the company, and that has them feeling unmotivated. Therefore, I think that, if they had some new goals for their business, it would motivate, and convince them to not retire yet. I believe that everyone else in the company falls under the reinforcement theory. The results that the engineers and the technicians give have no impact on them. If they try their best and make sure every product is perfect, they will get no pay raise or increase benefits. The same applies to them when they perform badly, and they make sure every product is defective, they will still make the same amount of money. This type of thinking is the reason why everyone else at the company is not motivated.

I think there are many ways the CEO and president can motivate their employees. One thing they can do is to introduce casual gaming in their office. Stress is tiring out workers and that can impact their performance significantly. Sometimes the stress of the workday can hurt employees' mental health, which can be very bad if left untreated. According to a study conducted by Educational Technology Research and Development, casual games in the workplace can increase attentiveness and motivate employees to work harder. "The current study, which examined learners' training behavior over a full year (12 months), suggests that a casual game may be played by the learner right before being provided instruction to enhance engagement with content and facilitate learning over a relatively long period" (Kapp, Valtchanov, & Pastore, 2020). Another solution that the CEO and president could implement would be monthly bonuses. These bonuses could reward the hardest workers with a prize of their choice. For example, if construction workers delivered the most parts in the month, they could choose what reward they want for the month. The CEO and president can survey to see what kind of prizes the employees would enjoy competing for.

Finally, the CEO and president could implement a commission-based salary and benefits. The employees are unmotivated because they know their results, and hard work does not matter. Why work harder if you are still going to be paid the same amount. Commission-based income could reward those who are working hard by giving them a paid upgrade. This would be great as people who were feeling rejected will be motivated again because they know their hard work will be rewarded.

Reference:

Koziol, L., & Koziol, M. (2020). The concept of the trichotomy of motivating factors in the workplace. Central European Journal of Operations Research, 28(2), 707–715. https://doi-org.libauth.purdueglobal.edu/10.1007/s10100-019-00658-5

Kapp, K. M., Valtchanov, D., & Pastore, R. (2020). Enhancing motivation in workplace training with casual games: a twelve month field study of retail employees. Educational Technology Research & Development, 68(5), 2263–2284. https://doi-org.libauth.purdueglobal.edu/10.1007/s11423-020-09769-2

APPENDIX I

Journal #4

Willy
Department of Management
MT 203: Human Resource Management
Professor M
November 7th, 2021

    It is unfortunate that we are in this situation but we have to make the most of it. There are many options that we can take that will help this company survive. The first we can do is cut the hours of our employees. This would prevent us from having to fire people and losing valuable employees according to information from the book (Noe Hollenbeck Gerhart & Wright, 2021, p.140). Another option we have is a hiring freeze. According to the book, (Noe Hollenbeck Gerhart & Wright, 2021, p.137), a hiring freeze would cut some of their expenses and the company doesn't have to lay people off. Lastly, we could lay off our workers based on how long they have been at the company. This process would allow us to keep our best employees and cut the cost for the company.

    Personally, I would prefer if we did the hiring freeze. When we cut people's hours, that will isolate the workers from us. Many will see it as a polite way of being laid off, and they will go pursue other jobs. By laying off people, we are risking the reputation of the business and any budding talent. It will leave the company to remain inactive, and we would slowly lessen. I understand that a hiring freeze would be stressful for our employees because they would have to pick up additional duties. However, it would allow any employee that still believes in our company the ability to stay, which could be the boost we need to get back on our feet.

Finally, out of all the options, I think that the hiring freeze makes a lot of sense for the company. Not only will it save the company money but also we don't have to lay off our workers. Even though the hiring freeze puts a lot of stress on the employees, it remains one of the best options for now until we pick up again moving forward.

APPENDIX J

Virtue Ethics is defined in the class as a "guide on what human beings are qualified to stand and on how they can develop patterns of good qualities that will naturally show them to their highest possibility." This kind of standard concentrates on how they can drive individuals to have more useful characteristics, such as habits, and dreams. For example, I like to be a better person, so I make sure I praise a spontaneous person every day. This is essential to me for two causes. One, I could brighten someone else's day and that makes me feel better as I am having an impact. Also, this habit will allow me to be nicer to people and become a better sociable person. In the case study, I believe Virtue Ethics would conflict with what the Volkswagen engineer was pushing. The engineer is developing a device that tracks the emission test of the state inspection. Virtue Ethics focuses on creating good habits to build the character of other people. This emission test ignores that as it is tricking people into considering a car is in better form than it is. It even constructs a bad habit for people as instead of resolving the situation, they assume that they can just use this device and it will fix all of their issues. By contrast, both the engineer and Volkswagen company did not adhere to the virtue ethics definition of the term or concept. Virtue ethics simply pledge the virtue and faithfulness of an individual. Moreover, it has to do with involving good conduct such as self-respect, goodness constitutes a fair and trustworthy person. It helps a person without a particular rule to transform the ethical complication.

Utilitarianism is another ethical theory that we discussed in class. Based on the information in the textbook, Utilitarianism is divided into two different parts. These two parts are Act utilitarianism and Rule utilitarianism. Act utilitarianism will focus on the impact of an action. For example, if I banned gummy bears from my town, how would that impact the happiness of the people living there? If the impact was bad for the overall happiness of the people living in the town, Act utilitarianism would remove the ban and focus on something that makes the people happy. Rule utilitarianism differs as it focuses on how good an action is for the people. For example, let's go back to the gummy bear example. If the gummy bears' band showed positive results in people's health, Rule utilitarianism would stick with the ban. In short, Act utilitarianism focuses on people's happiness, while Rule utilitarianism focuses on people's benefit. In this case study, I think both forms of Utilitarianism would have a different opinion. Rule utilitarianism would focus on the people's happiness, so if the people liked this device, they would not care about any of the positive or negative impactive. Act Utilitarianism would see the negative impact of this device and see that it could potentially get people hurt and would look to prevent this device from being made.

In transition, Utilitarians admit that the objective of integrity is to do good things by making life an exceptional experience for individuals around the globe. Utilitarians dismiss moral codes or rules that have to do with orders that are categorized by forms or structures handed out by authorities. In preference, utilitarians believe that what makes morality acceptable is its clear improvement to human beings.

Free market ethics is another ethical theory discussed in the book. Free market ethics is when companies focus on making a profit for their shareholders while obeying the law. Many people are not the biggest fan of this form because they are not moral, and it does not act in good faith. For example, a good example of this would be the EA sports user-term agreement. Many things are in the fine print such as the ability to take away games if they feel like they have done something wrong. Though this is not illegal, they know most people do not pay attention to the terms and agreements. Because of this, they are taking advantage of people's ignorance, which is very unethical. However, there is no law stating that they can't do this. People who believe in free-market ethics would push for the emission test device to go through if their shareholders liked the idea. As discussed above, there is no concern with safety or unethical practice when it comes to free-market ethics, there are only two things that matter: the law and the shareholders. If they aren't breaking the law, I think people who believe in free-market ethics would try anything as long as it makes their shareholders happy.

For example, if anyone is trading cigarettes, he/she could be betrayed of selling something noxious to health, but since their bargain is not forceful, it is not corrosive, therefore, not misguided. At last, utilitarian marketing would insist on giving a great service to customers, whether they pay a penny or more. Everyone deserves to be treated with respect and receives the assistance they need.

Footnote:

I believe that most people are trying to be fair and just in the eyes of others. Sometimes, they let themselves go by the temptation of money and fame. For example, a friend of mine started his career as a local politician. At first, he really cared about the people he represented in his district. Along the way, someone made him a huge offer financially that violated his ethics code of conduct. He chose money above everything else. Doing things like that hurts the people you love and certainly the ones that you represent in your district.

Resource:

Daly, D. J. (2021). Virtue Ethics and Action Guidance. Theological Studies, 82(4), 565–582. https://doi-org.libauth.purdueglobal.edu/10.1177/00405639211055177

Long, D. M., & Rao, S. (1995). The Wealth Effects of Unethical Business Behavior. Journal of Economics & Finance, 19(2), 65. https://doi-org.libauth.purdueglobal.edu/10.1007/BF02920510

Pereira, R. R. (2021). Virtue Ethics and the Trilemma Facing Sentiocentrism: Questioning Impartiality in Environmental Ethics. Environmental Ethics, 43(2), 165–184. https://doi-org.libauth.purdueglobal.edu/10.5840/enviroethics20215623

LIFE GOES BOTH WAYS

 I always feel fascinated by the Michael Jordan Nike commercial that goes like this: "Don't even think about it, just do it." Sometimes, it's better to take action rather than overthink things. Continually thinking about commencing a new project can hold up your progress in accomplishing your objectives. It's essential to retain a balance between planning and taking action to ensure success in your endeavors. The future is always uncertain, and we never really know what it holds for us. But even with all the unknowns, I believe that each of us has a mission and a reason for being here. It's up to us to discover that reason and make the most of the time we have. We may not be able to control the future, but we can control how we choose to live in the present. A powerful message goes behind that commercial. It's perfect not to keep thinking about starting a new project rather it would be better to jump head first and worry about the other stuff later. No one knows for certain what tomorrow will bring in your journey on earth. Sometimes I think we're all here for a reason, and it's up to each single person to find out what that reason may be and who knows what will happen if you trust your inner instincts and chase your dreams. If life is easy for certain people it's absolutely very difficult for most of us. No matter what is going on in your life you ought to remember that you're alone because other people are suffering just as much as you or worse. The beauty about all this is that, when you finally succeed in whatever you were afraid to do before, most of your pains would go away and everything else would become past-tense. The point of these analogies is to pass around some words of wisdom: Nobody is never too old, too smart or too little to learn from another person. We all have something unique or special about us we can teach them to others. In parentheses, when I decided to go back to school I wasn't completely sure how things were going to turn out (i.e., I had some doubts about failing specifically at my age). I took a chance by getting out of my comfort zone and eventually I accomplished what I wanted to do years ago. Moreover, with experience and times I noticed that most of the time things happened for a reason and at the right moment. If it was meant to be it would be (i.e., sometimes you can't force things to happen for you because it's not the time yet at least for you). The logic behind this theory is probably that there are some things we can't explain and they're beyond our imagination. I believe that there is a time frame and limit for all of us on this planet. You can do whatever you want to make things happen. The fact of the matter is, it will happen when the time is right. I am not trying to advance any argument, this is just an opinion based on my own experience and other individuals I come across in my life.

Footnotes:

Five or six months prior to my graduation at Purdue University Global I had the opportunity to work on an assignment for a class named Capstone 499. That assignment had everything to do with what I do for a living. First, I work in the financial industry as an Independent broker and most of my business is to help individuals with their financial needs. Indeed, the assignment was to develop a vision mission statement and it goes like this:

> A vision mission statement should be long-term and focus on the future. My vision statement is to be helping people with their financial problems and not only help them but make them much more successful doing that. Therefore, I need to make sure my financial skills are second to none. My dream for the future is to be a top-notch finical advisor. A financial advisor is someone who is in charge of saving people money and making them money. I hope I can take an average person in debt and turn them into a person who can create wealth for themselves! One thing I plan on doing is looking at various ways to make money. Making money is hard and I want to find the easiest way to do that for everyone. Therefore, I would research different types of investments and work to maximize the number of money people make. That way, I could recommend different advice depending on where a person is in

their financial journey. If I had to choose three different keywords to describe myself I would be: hardworking, relentless, and versatile. I am used to working very hard, balancing jobs and my family, so hard work is no issue for me. I make sure if I am working with a client to try my best and give them 100%. I am very relentless when it comes to finding solutions and working with people. I will not stop until I find a solution that works and satisfies everyone. I will use this quality to the best of my advantage and make sure each customer gets a great solution. Lastly, I am very versatile when it comes to dealing with people. I can deal with almost any situation because of my vast life experience. I would make sure everyone gets the best solution possible for their situation.

Right now, there are a couple of things I need to do to get the qualification for a financial advisor. First, I need to graduate from Purdue with bachelors in business. Next, there are several financial licenses I need to complete. For these licenses, there will be a couple of courses that I will need before I take these tests. I would also take many different financial courses on how to eliminate debt. This would be extremely helpful to my future clients, so I would make myself an expert on ways to delay/pay off debts as quickly as possible. Also, I would try to practice with friends to see certain tricks/advice that works and doesn't help. I would continue doing things like this for the next three years to sharpen my skills. I would also add different goals to make sure I am making progress that can be observed. My goals would be arranged in the short-term, mid-term, and long-term. My short-term goals would be: to finish up my bachelor's, talk to friends about helping them with their money problems, and register for classes to practice skills. My mid-term goals would be to: finish one license, help three friends with their financial problems and attend three courses to practice my skills. My long-term goals are: to set up my financial advisor office, get all needed licenses, and get my master's.

For my strengths and weaknesses, this is an excerpt from one of the journals we completed in class. I am a social human being; I enjoy others' company threefold. I am not a good fan of mediocrity. I take everything very seriously because I don't like to fail. I function best when challenges occur as I like to excel and emerge as a leader. I love to bring people together. Often my family and friends and bosses count on me to have the answers to details of an organized plan or something that is ready to go out all the way. I am very loyal and I try my best not to disappoint people who put their trust in me. I like to make things happen, and when others are clueless about a situation I always come up with a resolution that can accommodate them. I can work very well independently as well as in a group/team environment. I get along well with superiors, subordinates, and peers. As a financial services officer, I was very fortunate to work for two major organizations. I helped a lot of families reach their goals financially. Whether it was through life insurance or investment management I made a lot of individuals, families, and friends very happy. People trusted with their lives and some essential information about themselves. Information that their physician doesn't know about them. With the kind of work that I am doing this is just an opportunity to help others. Because of that, several of my clients developed a friendship with me. At the end of the day, I think that it is a good thing for individuals to trust you, particularly when you're in a position to help and can do just that when it comes to identifying and explaining each of my strengths or weaknesses concerning the knowledge, skills, and abilities required for each of the job opportunities. I would accommodate well because I am a great collaborator, a teacher, a fast learner, and a perfectionist. Thus, I believe in getting positive results as I can identify them as part of my strengths. Sometimes, I am too honest and have difficulty letting go of assignments until accomplishment. Other times, I am a little tough on myself at unfinished business. Finally, I am too analytical, which usually gives me a time frame to complete work. Finally, all these developments may be associated with weakness.

Resources:

Maulik, P. K. (2017, October 1). Workplace stress: A neglected aspect of mental health wellbeing. The Indian journal of medical research. Retrieved January 18, 2022, from https://www.ncbi.nlm.nih.gov/pmc/articles/PMC5819024/

Henry Inegbedion, E. S. (2020, January 10). Managing diversity for organizational efficiency—Henry Inegbedion, eze Sunday, Abiola Asaleye, Adedoyin Lawal, Ayeni Adebanji, 2020. SAGE Journals. Retrieved January 18, 2022, from https://journals.sagepub.com/doi/10.1177/2158244014019900173

APPENDIX K

"Motivation is a driving force thanks to which an entity undertakes efforts in the hope of achieving its objectives" (Koziol, L., & Koziol, M., 2020). If your employees are not motivated, there will be many consequences. The Timber Building Company is described as a business that builds and modifies offices. Lately, they have had issues that are widespread among the company.

One issue that the company has had is that the CEO and president are thinking of retirement. Another issue with the company is that their engineers are unmotivated and don't work as hard. The supervisor who is in charge of the production line and his technicians have been coming to work late.

This passage of information is from my previous assignment (Willy, 2022). "There are three motivational concepts people tend to focus on. These three are self-efficacy, reinforcement theory, and expectancy theory. According to the book (Robbins and Judge, 2019), the reinforcement theory is the idea that people will do things that lead to positive results and avoid things that bring negative results. In the book (Robbins and Judge 2019), the self-efficacy theory is defined as the ability to use goals to create positive behavior. Lastly, expectancy theory is almost the opposite of self-efficacy as effort will lead to the completion of goals based on information from the book (Robbins and Judge 2019)." These theories are important because they give us reasons why these employees are not motivated. By reviewing these theories, we can see where each employee falls under and find the reason why they are not motivated. For the CEO and president, I think their lack of motivation falls under the self-efficacy theory. They do not have any new goals for the company, and that has them feeling unmotivated. Therefore, I think that, if they had some new goals for their business, it would motivate, and convince them to not retire yet. I believe that everyone else in the company falls under the reinforcement theory. The results that the engineers and the technicians give have no impact on them. If they try their best and make sure every product is perfect, they will get no pay raise or increase benefits. The same applies to them when they perform badly, and they make sure every product is defective, they will still make the same amount of money. This type of thinking is the reason why everyone else at the company is not motivated.

    I think there are many ways the CEO and president can motivate their employees. One thing they can do is to introduce casual gaming in their office. Stress is tiring out workers and that can impact their performance significantly. Sometimes the stress of the workday can hurt employees' mental health, which can be very bad if left untreated. According to a study conducted by Educational Technology Research and Development, casual games in the workplace can increase attentiveness and motivate employees to work harder. "The current study, which examined learners' training behavior over a full year (12 months), suggests that a casual game may be played by the learner right before being provided instruction to enhance engagement with content and facilitate learning over a relatively long period"(Kapp, Valtchanov, & Pastore, 2020). Another solution that the CEO and president could implement would be monthly bonuses. These bonuses could reward the hardest workers with a prize of their choice. For example, if construction workers delivered the most parts in the month, they could choose what reward they want for the month. The CEO and president can survey to see what kind of prizes the employees would enjoy competing for.

    Finally, the CEO and president could implement a commission-based salary and benefits. The employees are unmotivated because they know their results, and hard work does not matter. Why work harder if you are still going to be paid the same amount. Commission-based income could reward those who are working hard by giving them a paid upgrade. This would be great as people who were feeling rejected will be motivated again because they know their hard work will be rewarded.

References:

Koziol, L., & Koziol, M. (2020). The concept of the trichotomy of motivating factors in the workplace. Central European Journal of Operations Research, 28(2), 707–715. https://doi-org.lib-auth.purdueglobal.edu/10.1007/s10100-019-00658-5

Kapp, K. M., Valtchanov, D., & Pastore, R. (2020). Enhancing motivation in workplace training with casual games: a twelve month field study of retail employees. Educational Technology Research & Development, 68(5), 2263–2284. https://doi-org.libauth.purdueglobal.edu/10.1007/s11423-020-09769-2

Footnote:

Lots of people underestimate the value of proper motivation. When someone is motivated I believe that he can overcome many different shortcomings in life. As an immigrant in the US, I have struggled with many different things such as the way of living, language barriers, and differences in culture. Over the years I met various types of people who didn't succeed despite being smart and talented. One thing some of them have in common is that they didn't have a good mentor. As an immigrant I had a feeling that I was going to be successful one day but I was not aware of how long it was going to take. Indeed, I can attest that the proper motivation is one major step towards becoming successful.

APPENDIX L

There are several reasons why orientation is extremely important to jobs. Many new employees are extremely nervous when it comes to their first day at work. Orientation helps ease these employees' nerves as they will not be working the traditional workday. Another great thing about orientation is it gets employees more work-ready. It gives them a preview of what the jobs are like and allows them to connect with their future coworkers. Lastly, it gives employers a chance to see their skills. Since another employee will be in charge of showing new employees around, he will see a couple of things. First, he will see what kind of skills the employee has and how well will he be able to handle the job. Once they figure out this, they can plan how to use the new employee. Because orientation is extremely important, it is vital to make sure you have the best orientation program to prepare new employees. The first thing my orientation would include would be an hour-long talk session with the other employees. It is extremely important to be comfortable with your coworkers, almost as important as the job itself. This will allow the new employee to get more comfortable with the job. Next, I would spend the majority of the orientation talking about the job. I will be telling them things like their job responsibilities, the skills needed for work, and how their day will look. The topics covered in the orientation would include: dealing with customers; different types of customers; our products; how the robot works; frequently asked questions; common issues; how to train customers; how to contact technical support, customer follow-up; dealing with unsatisfied customers. If any questions are asked, the question should be answered as thoroughly as possible to make sure the new employee understands. Next, I would spend the next hour showing him his other coworkers doing their job. I would explain what they are doing, why they are doing it, and how they are doing it. Lastly, I would show the new employee around the building making sure he gets familiarized with it. I would make sure I trained someone to conduct orientations and add an experienced employee. That way, they could answer any questions the new employee may have about the job. Orientation would be divided up into two days to prevent giving the new employee too much information at once. The orientation would be offered in two ways: in-person or online. We discussed in-person, but online would be handled a little differently. Online would be more information-based because it would be difficult to introduce employees from a web-cam/zoom. I would divide the online orientation into different sections and pack as much information as possible for it. I would include everything I discussed for the in-person orientation. I would even include a fun tour of the building and make it interactive so it doesn't get too boring for the new employee.

As the new human resource director, I will try my best to launch the company to a new elevation. The major issue that needs to be fixed is a new website. Nowadays, everything is digital and a majority of customers order through the website. With a boring and outdated website, we will be losing a majority of our potential customers. Websites are a large marketing connection and a great tool for any business. It doesn't matter how big or small your company is, your website is indeed one of the first perceptions you give. By creating a summary apparent to maneuver and revised view on the web, you will have the backing you need for many business undertakings.

The first time a client or customer enters your website, they should not have to do a lot of work to determine who the company is. Simply mentioning your name and summing up your products on the home page can avoid turbulence on both sides. You want to appeal to the interest of your observers within 2–3 seconds of them visiting your site so that they stick around to learn more about the business.

Another issue we have to deal with is the menu. The menu only satisfied one group of customers, which is the wealthier people. Our mission statement is "We provide healthy meals for all." We should try to focus on this because we are not meeting this statement. We need to add menu items and pricing that everyone can afford. One of the best ways you can continually reform your restaurant menu is with electronic signage. Lots of fast-casual restaurants are shifting toward this choice in order to save money on printing fees and grasp the compliance that shows up with digital make-happy. When you continuously reform the content with better and nicer designs and layouts it is easier to test different layouts that work at a reasonable price. Additionally, you can get rid of stocks that avoid customers' headaches and handle inventory. It is not necessary to keep breakfast, lunch, and dinner choices up all day. The menu content can be adjusted at any time of day.

The major factor affecting our employee turnover rate is our benefits. I have done some research to see what the average salary is in this industry. We offer the same salaries as them, which is good to attract workers. However, these other companies offer a lot more benefits than we do. At the moment, we only offer 2 weeks off every year, which is not good. By increasing the market rate salaries would be perhaps one standard solution. Adding personal time, healthcare incentives, bonuses, and stock options are excelling benefits that our company should consider on top of the two weeks off every year. It would be great to retain and attract existing and new talents to the company.

As the new HR director, I would bring more passion to the team. It is an excellent way to motivate the company but your staff are the ones responsible for selling the food, so you want them to be cheerful about the new menu. Host a private tasting between the servers, kitchen staff, head chef. Have the chef give his/her opinion about the ingredients and encouragement behind particular dishes. Not only will this enable your staff to be more familiarized but it allows them the freedom to choose their favorite dishes so that they can make reliable and concerned comments.

The definition of stakeholders is any individual or entity that has a crisis in an establishment. Stakeholders can have a powerful encounter with opinions regarding the process and financial matters of a company. Therefore, Stakeholders are investors, creditors, employees, and alike the regional community. The plant manager for

Ardnak plastic, Inc had three major problems to deal with, ethical, moral, and environmental.

In George's situation, he was dealing with the difficulty of increasing production while working with staffers setting confinements and sticking to government policies. George Mackee was working for a plastic parts company that produced an oil refinery. They asked George to govern their plant at Hondo but there was an industrialized pollution issue with the company.

The company's emissions difficulties transcend the EPA reports. Because of that, they were in jeopardy of paying fines if they redressed the problem. On one hand, Georgy's bosses were more concerned about making a profit versus fixing the issue. When the EPA found out different plants for the same company did not breach the EPA regulations they had more questions. Rather than do it during the day, these companies discharge their sub-standard emissions at night time when EPA inspectors are off duty. Georgy's superiors suggested that they should favor moving the plant to Mexico because the regulations are easy there, and EPA presence is absent.

In this scenario, George's bosses really don't care about the workers and the environment. As usual, these giant companies only care about profits and nothing else. When they move the company 15 miles from the US to Mexico, the pollution problems don't stop there. In fact, they're polluting two countries at once, the United States and Mexico. Another problem they face when they move the company to another country: What about the workers that have been working for the company for years or decades? How about their jobs, family, friends, and belongings? Aren't they significant? Yes, they are significant, and it is important to recognize the significance of everyone's contributions and efforts and compensate them accordingly for any troubles they may have faced. Fair compensation is crucial for maintaining a positive and productive work environment.

That is a decision that is going to have a huge impact on all the stakeholders. That is one way of explaining that these companies do not care about the result of their action as long as they make money. Some of them would falsify the rules or move to another country to avoid paying fines and disturb other people's lives. All these giant companies only care about money, and the bottom line is they would do it again. At last, policymakers should go forth with laws and regulations that make it more difficult for these businesses to act unethically.

Corporate social responsibility is company photography by which organizations make a collective attempt to work in ways that appreciate fairness rather than lessen society and the climate. CSR benefits both humanity and the description of businesses. Moreover, Corporate responsibility arrangements are a tremendous way to boost morale in the work area. Afterward, Corporate social responsibility is a self-regulating business illustration that aids an organization be culturally liable to itself, its stakeholders, and the public.

Bill was putting a lot of drive on George to come up with a resolution, or the company would be relocated to Mexico to avoid many legal problems. They violated the Clean Air Act of 1970.

That act looks after the stakeholders, modern and future origination from any harm from the air pollution, and commonly human beings are not able to notice with their eyes. EPA has a policy in place to encourage businesses to resolve their issues or amends. For the sake of the public, the moral standard and duty for George in this particular situation was to resolve the issue. That could have been an ethical thing to do. Businesses must take responsibility for any harm they may cause to the environment and to the people who inhabit it. In this case, George had a moral obligation to address the issue of air pollution and ensure that stakeholders, both present and future, were not adversely affected. It's important to note that hiding or ignoring the problem only makes matters worse and goes against the principles of Corporate Social Responsibility. As a manager, it was George's responsibility to understand the complexities of the situation and take appropriate action.

By law, companies are obliged to operate in ways that are going to protect the environment. Anything different from protecting the environment companies can be appealed and cited for a lot of money. At last, Arnad Plastic Plant has violated the "Clean Water Act." The acid rain and other kinds of stuff were contaminating the air and drinking water too. The act looks about to bring shelter to all origins of water, vegetation, marine life, and the ecosystem.

From an ethical point of view, George should have acknowledged the best interest of all individuals as he knows the right thing to do was to cut down the emissions. As for Bill, he tried to scare George. If the company does not stop gaining fines from the EPA they're going to move to Mexico. Georgy's decision was supposed to help the community move forward in a good way.

Bill had no right to ask George to react in a way that was going to help the company. Bill had no interest in the community or environment. He was only thinking about making the company some money without giving any thought to how this is going to affect the community financially.

The residents in the Hondo area have the authority to live happy, healthy, and free from any pollution that is going to harm their health. Additionally, George did not think about how his unethical behavior was going to affect future generations. The company ordered George to forge a selection that will breach the social and economic condition of a unified municipality. If George does not resolve the issue the company would move to Mexico. A lot of workers would lose their positions; therefore, the establishment would close as it would affect the economic situation of the residents of Hondo.

Finally, Ardnak Plastic Inc, located in Hondo, Texas, contravenes many environmental laws by permitting the discharge of pollution into the air. Because of that, the rights of the stakeholders were compromised. George had the opportunity to choose while advancing the issue as defined by the toxic violation codes. The right thing for George to do would be the ethical path. He should have inquired about a confrontation with Bill's boss and the board of directors to address the intimidation made to him and the town. If he was not satisfied with the results, he should have pursued legal counsel to help further with the problem. Despite everything, the company would have closed but George would have made an ethical decision. To cover up the issue is not the way to go as his decision will have a huge burden on people's health. The stakeholders trusted him to make the right choice and act ethically.

Resources:

Halbert, T., & Ingulli, E. (2017). Law and Ethics in the Business Environment (9th Edition). Cengage Limited.

Fraedrich, J. (2021, March 22). Https://kapextmediassl-a.akamaihd.net/healthSci/HA545/HA545_1703C/u5_as.pdf. Awascore.com. Retrieved May 3, 2022, from https://awascore.com/blog/https-kapextmediassl-a-akamaihd-net-healthsci-ha545-ha545_1703c-u5_as-pdf/

 Before we start this case, we must understand that balance sheet and income statement areas are very important here. The balance sheet is used to determine a value of a business, usually by listing things like the company's assets, liabilities, and owners' equity. These three things are vital to this case because they give us a good understanding of how well Pearson Air Conditioning & Service is doing. If their liabilities are higher than their assets, we know that the company is failing while the opposite is also true. An income statement is a little different from a balance sheet as it summarizes all the business's assets and expenses in a given period to figure out how profitable the business is. The income statement will help validate the balance sheet and also let us see how well Pearson has been doing in the given year. Using these two pieces of information together is important because it will give us a more accurate measurement of how the business is doing. For example, if the balance sheet shows the company has more liabilities than assets, we would assume that the business is failing. However, by reading the income statement, we learn that most of the company's assets have been generated in the past year. This tells us that the business is picking up and has a bright future ahead of it. We will be using information from these two sheets to determine many things and see how well of a company Pearson Air Conditioning & Service really is.

 Pearson Air Conditioning & Service is a business that is located in Dallas Texas. The two main people running the business are father and son, Bob and Scott Pearson. These two have two different roles. Scott Pearson is the company's president. In the text, a company's president is one of the highest positions in an organization and they are in charge of making sure certain things like the company's objective are being met. This is an extremely important position because the president is in charge of the company's future and the morale of its employees. For example, at my job, the company president makes sure of two things. First, he will research and create the company's realistic goals. Having impossible goals can run your business into the ground and destroy everyone's confidence, so he made sure he picked goals that were challenging but manageable. He would also make sure to keep an eye on employee morale as they were the lifeline of the business. He would often ask employees about any improvements that could be made to the company and he would try his best to make sure these improvements happened to the best of his ability. Bob Pearson is the company's general manager. Based on information from the textbook, a general manager is in charge of the company's daily tasks. To me, the general manager is often overlooked and it is a very important position. While the company president is in charge of creating the company's long-term goals, the general managers are maintaining their short-term ones. For example, the general manager at my job will work with the employees. He will give us tasks to complete based on our skillset and what is best for the day. The general manager is the one maintaining the business to make sure people like the president can complete their jobs. These two people are what maintain and drive Pearson Air Conditioning & Service to new heights. As a business, Pearson Air Conditioning & Service has its fair share of positive and negative aspects to their business. One good thing about this company has been the net profit. They were able to increase their net profit over the years and they currently have their highest amount of net profit. Another great thing about Pearson Air Conditioning & Service is their working capital. According to the book, a company's net capital is a company's asset minus its liabilities. Looking at the company's income statement, I was able to calculate that their current assets exceed their current expenses, netting a positive working capital. The major problem with Pearson Air Conditioning & Service is their inventory issues. The company seems to hold its inventory for up to 70 days, which is a very long time to hold. This time issue is especially worrying because most of their expenses have a time limit to pay off, which is 60 days. This is important because despite the business making money from their products, this money will take too long to come through as the expenses will need to be paid off. This issue could potentially eat away their profits and potentially lose Pearson Air Conditioning & Service all of their net profit.

    A company's assets are what determine its value of a company. The two major assets to check a business's worth in its accounts receivable and inventory. We discussed the inventory of Pearson above noting its strengths and weaknesses. Overall, they need to work on their inventory system to bring their potential expenses as it could be the reason Pearson Air Conditioning & Service fail as a business. For account receivable, there are good and bad things going on for Pearson Air Conditioning & Service. The account receivable account for Pearson has increased every year, meaning that they are gaining more assets and becoming more powerful. Another good thing about their account receivable is how they are handling bad best. In the textbook, bad debt is described as debt that cannot be recovered, however, Pearson has figured out a way they can use this to their advantage. In their balance sheet and income statement, the bad debt is reported as a loss for the company, which will reduce the penalty of the expense. Despite these good things, Pearson has a couple of issues regarding its account receivables. One major issue with their account receivable is their ability to pay off things instantly. Because they are holding their inventory for so long, they do not have immediate access to their cash. This could be a huge problem for the short/midterm because it prevents the business from affording their daily supplies/emergencies. Another weakness of Pearson's account receivable is the cost of maintenance. Pearson Air Conditioning & Service recently added a new inventory system to help them solve some issues that we mentioned above. One major disadvantage to this system is that it is computer operated and it requires a lot of maintenance. Things like computer costs and data storage can add up very quickly and may eat the potential profits that would be saved by using this new system.

When determining if a firm should reduce or expand the amount of its bank borrowing, you must know how to figure out the debt to equity ratio. According to investopedia.com, "The debt-to-equity (D/E) ratio compares a company's total liabilities to its shareholder equity and can be used to evaluate how much leverage a company is using." There is no number given to use on either the income statement or balance, but we do have both of the numbers needed to calculate it. The debt to equity ratio formula is taking the total liabilities and dividing them by the shareholder equity. The total liability is 136,211 and the shareholder equity is 126,625. By dividing these two numbers, we get 1.076. This is a good debt ratio as it shows that Pearson has been trying to grow more as a company by using debt to finance its activities. Despite this number being good, I would recommend that Pearson use more debt as they can afford it and it will bring their business to a new level.

I think Pearson Air Conditioning & Service is their working capital. They hold their inventory for too long because they are not able to sell everything and this has caused them to develop expenses that they did not account for. Pearson needs to pay off their debt quicker to avoid unnecessary fees, so I would propose that they keep with their inventory system. They should understand the demand for their products and figure out a solution that doesn't involve them holding their inventory. They also need to use their expenses better. According to the income and balance sheet, they are not using their expenses to their best potential. Pearson should have a cash discount, which is a reduction of an invoice based on the buyer and seller. Cash discounts are received when businesses pay off their debts earlier. With a cash discount, they would be able to purchase the equipment at a lower price.

Citation Page:

Longenecker, J. G., Petty, J. W., Palich, L. E., & Hoy, F. (2020). Small Business Management: Launching and Growing Entrepreneurial Ventures (19th ed.). Cengage.

Fernando, J. (2022, March 21). Debt-to-equity (D/E) ratio. Investopedia. Retrieved April 17, 2022, from https://www.

investopedia.com/terms/d/debtequityratio.asp#:~:text=Key%20Takeaways-,The%20debt%2Dto%2Dequity%20(D%2FE)%20ratio,with%20higher%20risk%20to%20shareholders.\

From an ethical business and moral point of view, these companies do not care about the result of their actions as long as they make money. Paying fines and property damage is only a small matter for them. All these giant companies only care about money, and the bottom line is they would do it again. One thing they should do is to advance laws and policies that make it harder for these organizations to act unethically. Breaking the law, endangering the lives of the public, and destroying the environment are simply unacceptable.

Corporate social responsibility is company photography by which organizations make a collective attempt to work in ways that appreciate fairness rather than lessen society and the climate. CSR benefits both humanity and the description of businesses. Moreover, Corporate responsibility arrangements are a tremendous way to boost morale in the work area. Afterward, Corporate social responsibility is a self-regulating business illustration that aids an organization to be culturally liable to itself, its stakeholders, and the public.

When organizations are conscious of their roles and the kinds of problems they will cause for future generations businesses will manage in ways that society and the environment would benefit from positively. For quite some time after the catastrophe, Amtrak's economic situation was out of bounds. They shifted from being in good standing in the market to contending with the other kinds of public transportation such as buses and airlines. They were well-positioned in that they could advance a broadly better fast form of travel than a bus and organize onboard fine dining. In addition, they could have projected a much lower rate of travel than an aircraft which does not have to consist of a meal of any structure. The organization felt the public tensions.

Frankly, this accident should have pushed the above conformity behavior fundamental to intrigue the economic solution of Corporate Social Responsibility. For instance, it would be extremely important to train and educate the conductors and their assistants including the pilots of the canal boats. Finally, Amtrak and Maravilla need to concentrate on their emergency action plans in case of an emergency as, by law, they are liable for the health and welfare of the workers and passengers in transit.

I feel like these companies do not care about the result of their actions as long as they make money. Paying fines and property damage is only a small matter for them. All these giant companies only care about money, and the bottom line is they would do it again. One thing they should do is to advance laws and policies that make it harder for these organizations to act unethically.

Breaking the law, endangering the lives of the public, and destroying the environment are simply unacceptable. If I were in charge of this company during the crash, there would be several things I would do. First, I would think about how this crash would affect the stakeholders. Before making any decisions, it's important to think about how these decisions would affect the stakeholders. People like the employees and the shareholders would impact my decision-making.

First, the employees would be properly trained and qualified to drive the train. Driving a train is something people spend a long time training before they are ready to drive it. So, I could not imagine how someone is capable of driving a train with inadequate training and experience. I would make sure all the train drivers have experience plus a six-month training course on how to operate the train. Second, I would see all areas this crash affected and try my best to make things right for the stakeholders. For example, this train crash negatively impacted the environment.

Thus, I would make sure the company is paying attention to environmental problems and try its best to make sure the business helps as much as possible. Lastly, I would apologize to everyone that was impacted by the crash. Moreover, I would have a shareholder meeting where I would take responsibility and personally apologize for jeopardizing their profit. I would have an apology letter sent to all of our employees and make sure I tell them everything about the case while taking full responsibility for my action. Lastly, I would try to hold a press conference by inviting anyone who is a customer or interested in the company. I would answer any questions that they had and in the end, I would apologize to everyone this may have affected. Finally, I would do the right thing by making sure everyone involved got compensated.

Lots of companies do not care about the result of their action as long as they make money. Paying fines and property damage is only a small matter for them. All these giant companies only care about money, and the bottom line is they would do it again. One thing they should do is to advance laws and policies that make it harder for these organizations to act unethically. Breaking the law, endangering the lives of the public, and destroying the environment are simply unacceptable.

If I were in charge of this company during the crash, there would be several things I would do. First, I would think about how this crash would affect the stakeholders. Before making any decisions, it's important to think about how these decisions would affect the stakeholders. People like the employees and the shareholders would impact my decision-making. First, the employees would be properly trained and qualified to drive the train. Driving a train is something people spend a long time training before they are ready to drive it. So, I could not imagine how someone is capable of driving a train with inadequate training and experience.

I would make sure all the train drivers have experience plus a six-month training course on how to operate the train. Second, I would see all areas this crash affected and try my best to make things right for the stakeholders. For example, this train crash negatively impacted the environment. Thus, I would make sure the company is paying attention to environmental problems and try its best to make sure the business helps as much as possible. Lastly, I would apologize to everyone that was impacted by the crash. Moreover, I would have a shareholder meeting where I would take responsibility and personally apologize for jeopardizing their profit.

I would have an apology letter sent to all of our employees and make sure I tell them everything about the case while taking full responsibility for my action. Lastly, I would try to hold a press conference by inviting anyone who is a customer or interested in the company. I would answer any questions that they had and in the end, I would apologize to everyone this may have affected. Finally, I would do the right thing by making sure everyone involved got compensated accordingly.

Corporate Social Accountability is extremely important to the company as well as the community. These activities can help the organization build a great rapport among workers and businesses. Also, this rapport can boost the morale of both workers and employers combined. At last. Everyone would feel linked to the sphere around them.

For a business to be culturally censurable it has to be liable to itself and its shareholders. Organizations that follow Corporate Social Responsibility designs have usually advanced their business in ways that they can share with society. Though, CSR is a strategy that's adopted by giant organizations. Finally, the more visible and successful a business is, the more bound it has to establish the basics of ethical behavior for its contemporaries, rival, and industry.

References:
Department of Labor Logo United States Department of Labor. About OSHA | Occupational Safety and Health Administration. (n.d.). Retrieved April 27, 2022, from https://www.osha.gov/aboutosha
Halbert, T., & Ingulli, E. (2017). Law and Ethics in the Business Environment (9th Edition). Cengage Limited.

Footnote:
As an individual who has been in different job's environments, I have seen various individuals do horrible things for money. This holds true for many big companies as well. Many of them would exploit their workers just for a quick buck.

Footnotes of reflection of the past:
It is my understanding that patience is one of the primary keys to success in life. If I could go back in time I would be more patient

than ever before. Learning to remain calm and patient comes with time, experience, and maturity. By all means, I am not trying to tell you that you should have a laid-back kind of attitude. What I am trying to tell you is not to force things in this life. Oftentimes stuff happens for a reason, whether the outcomes are positive or not we shouldn't ignore the fact that it wasn't meant to be. At times a lot of individuals are too reluctant to listen to their parents, and people that have been around before them. For instance, a very wise woman told me once, "There is no better adviser in this world than your father." The way I understand this adage is that it would be great if we listened to what our parents are teaching us. We will learn a lot more than we anticipated. Multiple times I wish that I could have another opportunity to relive my childhood journey with my parents and siblings. Things would be easier because I would have a better understanding of both life and them. I would be more obedient and cooperative.

Folks, our parents are like an unknown library awaiting to be discovered. They have information that we could really benefit from if we pay more attention to what they have to teach us. With all the knowledgeable wisdom that I accumulated over the years I wish that I could have another opportunity to be a kid again to live with my parents and my brothers and sisters. I think that I would be easier on them and they would love me more. After all, that's my imagination wondering about if I could have the opportunity to do it again I would have been able to do that…Then again we would never know about the outcome, and my point is this: we should not force things to happen for us in life; under circumstances some stuffs are already written down or meant to happen at a later time in life. Whether we believe it or not that is just the way it is.

Footnotes:

I loved to help out other people whether it was giving them advice or food. My dream was to go to medical school to become a doctor. I dreamt about becoming one of the best doctors who ever walked onto this planet. That part of life didn't happen; however, I became a financial officer instead. As pointed out, I am still able to help people reach their financial goals, and with all the financial knowledge and abilities that I have every time I have an opportunity to meet up with a new client, I make sure that he/she is in a better position financially than we previously met. It's a great feeling when you help someone.

Footnotes:

After high school graduation, my parents decided to send me to America for a better life. They didn't emphasize how hard it was going to be for me at 19 years of age. Going back I realized that I was tough-minded even though that bad experience left a terrible impression on me psychologically. If I were in my parents' position I would have never sent my kids abroad at that age. In a way, I am grateful to them for that experience but in another way, I am terrified inside my heart. Today if they're alive I know they would be extremely proud of what I have accomplished in school and my career. Because of all those preparations, I can raise my children better also, put them in a position to be successful in their lives. For one thing, they're all born in the USA and unlike me, they don't have to leave their country at that age in search of better opportunities. A lot of people don't know how fortunate they are to be an American.

For lots of folks coming from abroad to live in America for the first time it's like heaven on earth. I am confident that many of you would agree with me and also know for sure what I am talking about.

APPENDIX M

David Kolb was an American Educator. Though he was important for many different things, the thing people remember most about him was his learning cycle. According to simplypsychology.com, Kolb created this model in 1984 and made sure to publish his work to the public. Kolb's learning cycle is divided into four parts based on information from the textbook. The first part of his learning cycle was a concrete experience. This part of the learning cycle is somebody experiencing something for the first time by either watching it or doing it. For example, I had a concrete experience as a junior in high school when I experienced common core for the first time. This experience is important because it will have a big impact on the rest of the learning cycle. The next part of Kolb's learning cycle is reflective observation. This stage is reviewing the experience from the first stage. In this stage, you review what you learned and determine how you feel about it. For example, when I was learning how to play basketball, this stage was very critical to me. I would experience many things such as learning how to dribble, shoot and pass the ball. After I would experience these things, I would often go home and think about how everything felt. Why does the ball spin slow when I shoot or why does my crossover look different were thoughts I would have and I would continue thinking for the rest of the day. The next stage of Kolb's learning cycle is the abstract conceptualization stage. This stage comes after reflecting on your experience and you come up with ideas of how you will approach the next experience. For example, my mom makes some of the best macaroni I've ever had! My parents went on a long trip, so I got the chance to copy my mom's macaroni recipe. After making it, I was very disappointed with the results. After reflecting on how my macaroni was, I decided to come up with some solutions. Add more cheese, cook the macaroni for longer and add some paprika to the bread crumbs. I would continue thinking of new ways I could make my macaroni better and I created a list of things that could potentially make my mac & cheese better. The Last stage of Kolb's learning cycle is active experimentation. This stage is where the ideas from the third stage are put into action. Instead of just thinking of new ways to make things better, this stage is focused on doing things to see if they impact anything. For example, with the macaroni and cheese I made, I decided to put everything I was brainstorming into effect. I added more cheese, cooked it longer, and added some paprika. The end result was better than the first macaroni and cheese, but there was still a lot of work to be done. This cycle would continue for me as I experienced many different forms of macaroni and cheese. This is the same for people who are learning new things. They experience something for the first time and reflect on that experience. They think of ways they could improve that experience and they experiment by putting these ideas into action. Once these ideas are executed, the learner experiences a new thing again and the cycle continues.

If I had to describe Kolb's learning cycle to people who weren't familiar with it, I would describe it as a science experiment. With science experiments, you will try to solve an issue that no one else has solved. This is the same as you experiencing something for the first time. Once you go through with this experiment, you have to think on how your experiment went and think if there was anything you missed. This is very similar to learners reflecting on their first experiences. After the experiment, scientists will have to brainstorm ways they could improve the experiment to make it more accurate. This is the same thing as learners thinking of new things they could do to improve the experience they had. Lastly, scientists will put these new ideas into their new experiment, while learners will use their ideas into the next experience. Both of these groups of people will also repeat this cycle and continue to make progress towards it.

APPENDIX N

There are many problems that the world is dealing with. One problem is that the world is dealing with its environmental problems. These problems include things like pollution, climate change, deforestation, and loss of biodiversity. These are problems that could affect our daily lives and if we are not careful could lead to the end of human society. One of the biggest contributors to environmental problems would be businesses. Because of this, there are a group of people who are focused on observing these problems and trying to come up with solutions. These groups of people are called environmentalists. Environmentalists are extremely important to our society because they are trying their best to make sure these problems are solved. One of the most important environmentalists would be Paul Hawken. Paul Hawken is an environmentalist that decided to focus his entire life on stopping these issues from happening. The fruits of his work would be his eight principles. Many believe that these objectives are the eight objectives. Hawken states that if each person were to follow these eight objectives, we would be able to solve all these environmental problems and a whole bunch of other different problems.

One of the first objectives Hawken brings up is to reduce absolute consumption of energy and natural resources in the North by 80% within the next half-century. The first thing we can break down is the use of the word the north, meaning mostly the United States. In 2016, there was a study conducted comparing each country to find out how much energy each country is using. To do this, they measure each country's energy consumption by British thermal units. According to the EIA, "A British thermal unit (Btu) is a measure of the heat content of fuels or energy sources. It is the quantity of heat required to raise the temperature of one pound of liquid water by 1 degree Fahrenheit at the temperature that water has its greatest density (approximately 39 degrees Fahrenheit)." The world as a whole used about 572.8 quadrillion British thermal units. The US used about 97.5 quadrillion Btu, which based on americangeosciences.org accounts for 17% of the world's energy consumption. Meaning that to decrease the world's energy consumption, the US should be the first place we should target.

There are many ways we can decrease energy consumption. The first thing we could do would be to offer better energy consumption appliances. Many of the appliances that we own use way more energy than they should and many different alternatives use up less. If we were able to replace all of these appliances with their more fuel counterparts, we would be well on our way to decreasing energy consumption. Another thing that we could do would decrease our dependence on fossil fuels. There are many sources of energy that could replace fossil fuels. Biomass, Hydrogen, and Biofuels are some of the few energy that could replace fossil fuels. These two solutions would help bring down energy consumption until we can get down 80% as Hawken mentioned.

The second objective that Hawken mentions is to provide secure, stable, and meaningful employment for people everywhere. This is important because this is a very underrated part of life that consumes lots of energy. For example, my dad drives to New York City every day for work. This is about a 1-hour drive, not counting things like rush hour traffic and accident jams. During this time, the car will be burning fuel from things like gas consumption, heating, and more. Many people have to drive a long way to work, increasing their energy consumption day by day. If there was a stable employment place that would be town to town, there would be no need to drive so far. Because there would not be as many people driving each day, the energy consumption would drop down considerably. This would also stop people from driving to look for employment opportunities as there would be in their town.

The next objective that Hawken talks about is to be self-actuating as opposed to regulated or morally mandated. This is the first that addresses the people of the US, rather than the US as a whole.

Hawken is saying that people need to think of ways they can decrease the use of their energy consumptions, rather than depending on the government or other people to solve it for them. I agree strongly with Hawken's point here and think that we also have a responsibility to decrease energy consumption. There are many ways that we can decrease energy consumption. One way that we could decrease consumption would be to unplug electronics that are not being used. Many people do not understand that plugging in electronics will use energy, regardless of whether you are using it or not. By unplugging things we aren't using, we are saving countless amounts of energy. Another simple thing we could do is buy an energy-saving device. Items like ovens, computers, and heating devices have products that use less energy than normal ones. Buying these products would save a lot of energy, so try your best to get them.

The next objectives of Hawken are to honor market principles. When Hawken states that we should honor market principles, he is stating that we should use agreed-upon marketing techniques when trying to sell products to customers. This is important because new marketing tactics could lead to new problems. For example, monopolies are not a marketing principle that people agree upon. Monopolies can lead to problems beyond the business world such as factories and pollution. Monopolies are also bad for consumers because they increase the price of goods while lowering the quality of goods. Market principles are a guideline people should follow because they are things that people already agreed upon.

In his objectives, Hawken also stated that we should be more rewarding than our present way of life. Being more rewarding is an objective that is geared towards the people rather than the country. I think what he is saying here is that by being more rewarding than you are now, you can solve a lot of problems. For example, if I apply this line of thinking, I would be kinder to other people. If I am kinder to people, other people will also be kinder to me. Because there is this cycle of kindness, people, in general, would cause fewer issues. It would destroy problems that were caused by jealousy or misunderstandings.

The next thing that Hawken states are to exceed sustainability by restoring degraded habitats and ecosystems to their fullest biological capacity. This is one of the big parts of his objectives as it states that we must try and rebuild environments. This is an issue bigger than the US and the whole world should focus on doing this. There are many ways we can start rebuilding destroyed habitats. One way we can do this is by replanting forests that we destroyed. This is big as we are losing too many forests and are on the path of losing them for good. By replanting these forests, we are encouraging the growth of habitat species and new natural resources. Another thing we should do is decrease pollution. This Is huge because this is one of the main reasons why so many habitats are being destroyed. Wildlife can take the pollutants, so they either move on or die. By reducing pollution, we will allow these habitats to rebuild themselves and prevent future habitats from being destroyed.

The second last objective on Hawken's list would be to rely on current income. I believe there are two reasons why Hawken states that we should stay on our current income. The first would be to solve inflation issues. If prices rise, people are forced to get more jobs and the cycle continues. If people rely on their current income, the goods people are selling will not be bought. Because of this, the price of goods will decrease, solving any problems with the rising inflation rates. The other reason why Hawken states we should rely on our current income is environmental issues. If people are looking for more job opportunities, they are using their cars and burning fossil fuels. This is bad for the environment as it creates pollution and burns more energy. To solve this, Hawken believes we should rely on one source of income, which would stop both things from happening. Relying on one source of income would also lead people to be less stressed out, and that would create fewer problems.

Lastly, Hawken states that we should be fun and engaging, and strive for an aesthetic outcome. Out of all the objectives, I think this one is the most important. People become stressed out easily, thus are not happy with their lives. Becoming stressed out can lead to some major problems. For example, a friend of mine became stressed out as he was dealing with a bunch of issues. Because of this, he

LIFE GOES BOTH WAYS

would continue to make decisions that would impact his life in a negative way. One way we can become less stressed is by having fun. In the example I mentioned above, my friend would solve his issues by creating a new hobby, which was playing volleyball. He is doing great for himself and even quit his job to become a professional volleyball player. By having fun, you will be much happier in your life, which will create fewer problems for everyone else. If everyone were to make their lives funner, they would live better lives and make the world a better place.

There are many issues in our world. Some of these issues include environmental and problems with our daily life. Hawken's eight objectives offer a way we can solve these problems. By following these objectives, we can make the world better for us and future generations.

APPENDIX O

"Business strategy is defined as a guideline for a company to market its products and services to the best of its abilities. Because company strategy is so important, many other institutions employ different ideals and views depending on their industry and several other factors. One example of how complex business strategies can be is the Porter's Diamond Model. According to decisionstats, Porter's Diamond Model explains that some businesses have an advantage because of the country they are in. It explains why some countries preserve prospering enterprises that different countries don't carry such as oil in the middle east.

"A good company to look at in terms of business plans would be Apple. It is a technology company that concentrates on selling various products. Some of the products Apple offers are iMacs, AirPods, and iPhones. Their company strategy is product differentiation. This means that Apple centers its business on the exceptional products they sell. This functions for them because their customers love their products. When it's time to buy their products they have to get them from Apple."

This strategy never changed but the products Apple offered were different. Instead of iPhones and iMacs, Apple focused on selling products like iPods and mp3 players. They targeted a different type of market and were more of a niche company. They did not change their strategy but changed the market they were targeting.

According to the Apple product page, its vision statement is "Apple strives to bring the best personal computing experience to students, educators, creative professionals, and consumers around the world through its innovative hardware, software, and internet offerings." Apple is a big advocate of education as they donate products to many different schools. Because of that, Apple is following its vision statement. Apple's mission is to give its customers the best products in the industry and a great experience while using these products. Apple is following its vision statement based on the products like the iPhone and iMac. Based on information from their website, Apple values privacy, racial justice, protection of the environment, and education.

Apple's objective is part of its mission statement, which is to deliver the most unique products on the market. They are doing a fantastic job as they have products that their competitors do not offer. Their competitors are all technology businesses such as Google, Microsoft, and Samsung. None of these companies offer anything like the iPhone or a subscription service like Apple music. Therefore, Apple is very close to completing its objective. Companies need to have strategic initiatives. Strategic initiatives are ways companies can maintain their goals and turn them into reality. Apple is great at doing these as they have taken product ideas and turned them into products. For example, AirPods is a great example of Apple's strategic initiatives. The idea of Bluetooth headphones is not new, but they were usually bulky and hard to work with. Apple changed this with the introduction of their new product, AirPod. These were very small, very comfortable to use, and worked very well. They were able to take their goal of creating new products for a more satisfactory customer adventure and they turned that into a new product.

Apple is excellent in terms of operational excellence. According to the book, operational excellence is a way that companies create a culture in their workplace. They can hire the best people in their field. They think of new products and different ways to improve their current product. Apple offers many different benefits to its employees while paying a competitive salary. The management body is very important for Apple as they stand accountable for the product concepts. The governance body is at the shelter of the business such as the highest leadership or board of directors. They decide what kind of products they want to focus on and discuss any new ideas that they decide to execute. The latest idea that Apple selected to focus on was enhancing their AirPods, which was a huge victory for them.

ABOUT THE AUTHOR

Willy Vil is a father of three wonderful boys. He's been married for over two decades. He is a loving and dedicated father, and he also cares deeply about his family. He will do anything for his family, especially to help his children move ahead in their lives. He is a successful entrepreneur as he has a bachelor's degree in business administration with a concentration in management. He went to Purdue University Global, where he was an exceptional student and he graduated with honors.

In his spare time, he loves to watch action movies and listen to his favorite R&B songs from the '70s and '80s. Willy V. is an outstanding handyman, and now and then, he likes to start a new project by fixing things in the house. He has fixed the place from top to bottom. He has a great sense of humor and is an ideal person to be around. Anybody can learn from him a few things. Moreover, he loves luxury cars from Europe and Japan.

He loves sports as he likes the New York Knicks, the New York Giants, and the New York Rangers. If time permits, he would go to one of the stadiums with his boys to watch his favorite team. Willy V. enjoys swimming on warm beaches and also loves traveling to different countries to experiment with their food and learn about their culture.

Printed in the USA
CPSIA information can be obtained
at www.ICGtesting.com
CBHW021436061024
15371CB00039BB/554